Seven Days

Nathan Munday originally comes from a small village in Carmarthenshire but he now lives near the Gabalfa Interchange where he has surrounded himself with lots of books. Doing a PhD means that he has to escape to the mountains at least once, or maybe twice, a year. He won the M. Wynn Thomas New Scholars Prize (2016) and came second in the New Welsh Writing Awards (2016). This is his first book.

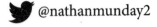 @nathanmunday2

Seven Days

Nathan Munday

PARTHIAN

Parthian, Cardigan SA43 1ED
www.parthianbooks.com
First published in 2017
© Nathan Munday 2017
ISBN 978-1-912109-00-5
Editor Gwen Davies
Cover design by Robert Harries
Typeset by Alison Evans
Printed by Pulsio
Published with the financial support of the Welsh Books Council British Library
Cataloguing in Publication Data
A cataloguing record for this book is available from the British Library

I fy chwaer

Cassini family, Luchon, Bareges, Bagneres (1781)

Prologue

In the beginning God created the Pyrenees. And the hills were without form and void; and darkness was on the face of the cliffs. Everything begins in the dark. The absence indicates an imminent presence which is hiding in the void. At night, it's like being there at that Genesis moment hearing echoes of somebody speaking existence. The wind is like the brooding Dove slowly shifting the darkness through the valleys. As I walk, the silence is disturbed by a crooked line on the horizon. It rises. Echoes become sounds as huge tectonic plates grind one another, pushing the mountains up. At first it looks like teeth before changing into a row of books leaning on one another in an old chain library...

Robert Macfarlane wrote that 'most religions operate on a vertical axis [...] to ascend, therefore, is in some fundamental way to approach divinity'. In the secular world too, 'to peak' has become a symbol for endeavour and human accomplishment. There is something very appealing about going uphill. In 1336, Petrarch and his brother Gherardo climbed that Provençal hill called Ventoux 'to see what great an elevation had to offer'. It is not a high hill like some of its southern and eastern siblings; Ventoux is only 1910m above sea level. Petrarch recorded his hike in a letter, probably written by candlelight in the mountain inn, to Dionisio da Borgo San Sepolcro where he notes how, in that single day, he had raised his soul, as he had done with his body, to higher places. He was overwhelmed by the view:

> *As if suddenly wakened from sleep, I turned about and gazed toward the west. I was unable to discern the summits of the Pyrenees, which form the barrier between France and Spain; not because of any intervening obstacle that I know of but owing simply to the insufficiency of our mortal vision. But I could see with the utmost clearness, off to the right, the mountains of the region about Lyons, and to the left the bay of Marseilles and the waters that lash the shores of Aigues Mortes, altho' all these places were so distant that it would require a journey of several days to reach them. Under our very eyes flowed the Rhone.*

This book documents my seven days on that barrier between France and Spain. In a way, I imagine both me and my father mirroring Petrarch and his brother. If my mortal vision was better, I may have been able to see Ventoux in the distance and we would have waved at the poet and his brother who, in my mind, are always sitting on its bare peak. He is a father-figure to so many writers who like going uphill. But we are mortal and I must leave such imaginings to what Macfarlane calls the mountains of the mind, rather than the real Pyrenees: 'What we call a mountain is thus in fact a collaboration of the physical forms of the world with the imagination of humans – a mountain of the mind.' Those mountains have other figures on them too. This is a book in dialogue with the greatest book ever written – the Holy Bible – as well as a return to the iconic mountains which can be climbed in that book. The Bible is full of hills, peaks, and high places which have always fascinated me. *Seven Days* explores those heights where the extraordinary communes with the ordinary and where the lower things of earth grow strangely dim.

Seven Days is also a thank you to all the storytellers who have made my first twenty or so years very full and exciting. That particular week seemed much longer and yet each mountain trip we made before and afterwards seems to fuse into that single week where the whole world was under our eyes. In B*lack Apples of Gower: Stone-Footing in Memory Fields*, Iain Sinclair wrote that the 'walks that truly haunt, and hurt, are the ones that walk you'. In my mind, the crooked lines on any horizon always take me back to that ridge just below Spijeoles and every ascent takes me back to that particular snowy climb a few years ago.

~

Dad and I are nearing a Pyrenean *Eilean a 'Cheò* (Isle of Mist). The mist is a sea and the hills appear like those Misty Isles that Ossian saw growing in the distance as he sailed towards Skye. I cannot quite see the shoreline yet but I am anticipating archipelagic hills. At the moment, I can't see anything. Going down would be easier and quicker, but going up is always rewarding.

The sun. At last. The misty sea breaks onto the shore of a hill. Sunlight quickens the stone and breathes life into the whole area. The mountain transports us to the beginning, demanding that we face the shadows of some unutterable holiness. It feels like I'm the first man on earth. Everything is fresh and new. I am exposed. The sound of our clanking ice axes disturbs that silence and echoes around the cirque. I look around – the massif presents itself – an unfinished cathedral, with the mark of divine stonemasonry scraped into its cliffs.

Ahead of me is my father. I study him. A *Pyreneist*. The rhythmic guide of the axe sets our walking tempo like a metronome. One minute he is a climber with a strange trust in the hill, and the next minute, he is an old-fashioned pilgrim – an unfamiliar phantom wanderer; he looks lost, but he is not. He stops when a chamois or an isard (*Rupicapra pyrenaica*) appears. Everything is so still. Perhaps she is one of *Culhwch and Olwen's* Oldest Animals, another *Carw Rhedynfre*?

That old stag witnessed the life span of an oak tree but had never heard about the son of Modron. This creature is not a stag, but her marble, amber eyes are pensive and mature. The brown curves of her body move elegantly across the rocks.

A slight slip causes one of the rocks to tumble. She stops. I gaze at her horns before being drawn down to her eyes again. We look at one another. I am no Gwrhyr and I cannot speak her language.[1] By the time the rolling rock is still, she has disappeared.

We are getting higher. A snowy ramp comes into view offering us a straight passage towards the col.[2] I can't be bothered to put my crampons on because the snow looks safe enough. The rim is haloed by bright light; flickers trick my eyes and create a personal aurora borealis.

'I'll kick some steps,' Dad says. He kicks the mountains' cheeks, making steps with his hard boots. I plod up the steep bit, foot by foot. Kick, kick, snow flying, ice, crunch, step, step… something like that, as we ascend in a zig-zag towards the col.

---

1 Gwrhyr Gwalstawd Ieithoedd was one of Arthur's knights in *Culhwch and Olwen*. He was a shapeshifter and could speak every language including the languages of birds and animals.
2 Col – The lowest point on a mountain ridge between two peaks.

I'm falling
  the first thing to do is to
  plonk
    this ice axe in the ice
      once   rubbish   I've missed
        I'm speeding up
          quicker again,
            no I've missed and cut myself by missing—
            I'm bleeding. I'm only nineteen.
            Quicker.
              I'm going to die.
                I'm not going to graduate. Unbelievable!
                Third time. Here we
                  go.
                    Lord, have mercy!
                    Crack!

The fiery alp on one side has stopped moving whilst the hill I'm on has grown overwhelmingly large. My arm hurts. The snow has burnt and blistered the area between my elbow and wrist. My father slowly comes to a halt before turning around. He takes a long time to descend but, at last, he is familiar again.

~

Two years go by and we decide to return to the mountain.

The Route up Pic de Spijeoles

Rue Bonjour Map

I will lift up mine eyes unto the hills,
from whence cometh my help.
My help cometh from the Lord,
which made heaven and earth.

Psalm 121

The earth strains to contain the Word-breathed life.
The mountains roll out their shadows across the plain
like long black canvases. The ground itself seems to
quake under the light. Gaps and holes are on the verge
of producing something. They wait for instruction like
runners anticipating a cracking gun. Suddenly, the
ridges evolve from two-dimensional teeth into three-
dimensional puzzles jumbled up in a perfect order. The
master mason weathers the cliffs and grinds the peaks:
spices in a mortar. The lightning, the wind, the heat,
the ice are pestles; they pound and paint the landscape
with power. Only then can the sweet aroma be pleasing
to both future mountaineers and that great maker who
orchestrates the scene from the circle of the earth.

Everything begins in the dark. Seven days began in a
car park and our headlights spotted figures setting up
tourist stalls along its periphery. The air was cold, the
sun young and transparent, whilst muffled shouts of

tradesmen disturbed what had been a hushed journey. Breakfast relics adorned the car floor: a Tropicana bottle and the remains of a flaky croissant that had fallen like confetti. It got lighter. This magic twilight attracted our morning gaze. Big shapes started to appear in the distance as the sun intensified like the top of an emerging lighthouse. I could see cliffs. I could see peaks. The car park was clearer too. This piece of asphalt, this simple car park, marked the beginning of the 'Rue Bonjour', a popular tourist track named after the thousand greetings that you'll probably give and receive whilst walking along it.

Our first destination was the Refuge d'Espingo (1967m), a mountain refuge situated at the end of the Rue Bonjour between Lakes d'O'ô and d'Espingo under the shadow of Pic des Spijeoles. I had been there before. We used it as a base when I first attempted Spijeoles two years ago. Whenever I think of that place, I remember one bloke in particular. Cue Rachmaninov's vespers. He was the spitting image of Rasputin. We came round the corner and he was sitting there, in the doorway, smoking a cigarillo with his wife leaning like an apostle on his shoulder. He was big and strong and his eyes were glowing. At night, you would see him perambulating around the lake and he would look over as if he'd spotted you. Creepy. Anyway, Dad had been to the Refuge d'Espingo often. I imagined Dad arriving at the place time after time, crossing the threshold, wearing different coats and hats, whilst his hair got greyer and greyer.

The tradesmen were hurrying around, selling cheeses, wines, shepherd sticks, and sheep-shaped moccasins that bleated as you passed them. The half-light was filling with the sound of fake flocks, clicking cameras and weary youths emerging from VW camp-ervans with Gromit-like eyes, their breathing creating cumuli like the pale breath of cattle. From the belly of the van I heard 'Like a Rolling Stone'. It was Dylan. The harmonica wheezed as the door rolled shut; they were going back to bed. I didn't blame them. The mountain held our imagination as in a shadow. I could not see it physically but it loomed like a spectre in my mind, still snow-capped and mysteriously un-climbable.

Back in the car, Dad was wearing one of his strange hats. I can't remember exactly which one, but it was either the Bob Marley colourful hippy hat from his student days or his Afghan Pakol hat; these are his two favourites. He went to a funeral once in his Pakol hat and a tie with loads of giraffes walking across its black. Mam went crazy when she met us at the church gate, grabbed the hat like a lioness, and threw it into the gutter. He gets a lot of his clothes from Oxfam or the Green charity shop in Llandeilo much to my mother's dismay. I don't buy clothes there but I have acquired some good books which seem to have been left to me by dead preachers and rich farmers. We sat in the car for a bit in front of the heater. Dad was wearing his hat whilst I lingered in the warm air, seeking the imminent sun. We must have looked like a pair of caged birds, perched in a Skoda Yeti.

I was grateful that I had not died two years before. I can remember lying on the hill and thinking 'what a steep angle' before feeling incredibly relieved to find that I was still alive. There are many ways of dying in the mountains and this was not a particularly dangerous place. Mountain-worship demands sacrifice. In the summer of 1997, 103 people were killed in seven weeks in the Alps. I do not know how many people die in the Pyrenees but I remember thinking 'how embarrassing it would be if I died here; this is no Matterhorn!' But later I read Edward Whymper's words which challenged me:

> *Climb if you will but remember that courage and strength are naught without prudence, and that a momentary negligence may destroy the happiness of a lifetime. Do nothing in haste; look well to each step; and from the beginning think what may be the end.*[3]

Whymper's words could have been uttered by a preacher. There is something deeply religious about climbing. To me as a child, the Bible was never boring.

3 Edward Whymper, *Scrambles amongst the Alps* (1871). Whymper (1840-1911) was an English mountaineer who is best known for the first ascent of the Matterhorn in 1865.

I can remember being drawn to the rugged mountain-top scenes, following scrambling prophets in my mind, and touching cairn-like altars surrounded by alpine vistas. I can remember traversing through the old picture Bible. The blonde blue-eyed Jesus stood on a peak like Edmund Hillary and the devil fell away without a rope. One picture was even more vivid. I used to peep before turning the page. It portrayed the prophet Jeremiah who had been thrown down a deep, dark well like Joe Simpson down that crevasse near Siula Grande. The sides were rocky and cliff-like and his eyes seemed so far away. That picture haunted me. At night, I would imagine falling down that well and losing my feet to frostbite. I would then look up and see the opening – a distant moon. Eventually, I laid the old picture Bible aside and delved into the words instead. I found that some of the most important accounts are located in the higher places. The blonde blue-eyed Jesus metamorphosed into someone real and familiar. The words drew a Jewish carpenter with rough hands and kind eyes – still a keen mountaineer. The devil's horns and red hued skin disappeared too; he changed into something much more frightening: Lucifer, that angel of darkness decked in light. Jeremiah was always the same though: down a hole and waiting for a rope.

As I got older I noticed how Dad – a Christian and a climber – also used religious language in both contexts. This language is usually channelled, like Whymper for example, through that eschatogological fascination with destinations, ends, outcomes, and judgements.

'If we don't get going soon, we'll be too late. The light is dimming' or 'treat the mountain carefully, or you'll never reach the end', 'Get off before four or you'll be punished' – all that kind of stuff is a long way from the 'hills are alive with the sound of music.' I guess the mountains have a long playlist though.

Mountains have become synonymous with life and death. Pyrenean *tabacs* herald conquests as well as defeats, bearing sad news headlines in shop windows where the glue from each ghostly piece of paper leaves gummy smudges on the pane. There is nothing worse than seeing a sad news headline before starting your day. The locals' faces tell the story of every mountain. They look up and say nothing. Their eyes reveal the character of the hill whether he is deadly, welcoming, tricky, mystical or just plain impossible. It is at this point that the various shrines, and the entire religious lingo, start making sense. When I stepped out of the car, I noticed a shrine with a shrunken Virgin Mary in it. She was dressed in blue, her hands were Dürer-like and flowers surrounded her dress. Indeed, most of the paths are littered with little shrines containing statuettes of the Virgin, or some local saint, with their eyes uplifted, pleading with God for mercy. It is a shock when a natural landscape of pale blue sky, and grey mountains dabbed by fresh white is disturbed by a crucifix. One minute there is a Swiss panorama, and then, a life-size statue crosses your gaze. Usually the sunken eyes and the half-opened mouth depict an unreal beautiful young man. Christ on the cross! These porcelain anachronisms might be mistaken in the half-light for mountain martyrs, hung out to ward off those who would venture up the higher slopes. The still, deadly hush in each Jesus figure reminded me of the broken bodies of those heroic climbers, fallen dead. They say that mountaineer George Mallory's body was relatively unbroken when they found him on the North Eastern Ridge of Everest in 1999. These shrines or crucifixes always disrupt the landscape with macabre stillness. It is easy to forget that the Christian religion worships a risen Saviour when you see him dying on every corner.

Religion is moulded, and moulds itself, to a particular context. The church and cattle bells are usually indistinguishable while the sacred buildings merge with the grey cliffs from whence they came. The silence – associated with the hill – can be both a comfort and a fear; in a way, these two words are very apt when something draws our awe. It is then that you realise that the statues' eyes are not directed towards God but they gaze at the hillsides. Peaks are deified whilst the Virgin of the Scree is located on every corner. Yes, the mountain, in all its majesty, is a god of stone which some bow to, talk to, and ultimately, give their lives to.

A Shrine to the Virgin Mary

In the corner of the car park a young climber sat on the wall. He ran his purple rope through his fingers like a rosary. I think he was checking it carefully before beginning his trip. I noticed a yellow Tibetan prayer flag flapping from his rucksack. His eyes were closed and he was enjoying his fellowship with the warming sun. Meanwhile, Dad was putting his round aviator glasses on which made him look like a cross between Biggles and John Lennon. He always takes the preparation very seriously and a strange hat with odd glasses seems to be a ritualistic must on every trip.

'The bags are heavy... It's the blasted food', he made a face as he jumped up and down with his rucksack on.

'It'll be okay.'

'You say that now.' As we were preparing, the young climber had already walked two hundred yards up a quieter valley path.

'Pity we can't go that way,' I pointed at the boy with the purple rope.

'Yes I know. He's doing something technical. I don't actually know where that goes,' he turned and looked at the approaching bus, 'Unfortunately, we've got those brats to look forward to for the first hour.'

Dad frowned at a bus full of gargoyle-faced schoolchildren who were eyeing the surrounding solitude for sonic conquest. 'We've got to get going.' He picked his Leki stick like a warrior girding himself for battle and started walking before the children could even un-clip their seatbelts.

I looked up at the hills that bordered the path and there was still some snow. The mountains seemed grumpy and aloof. Ever since the fall, I do not climb a snowy slope in a T-shirt. I am more prudent. I cover my skin like my sister did as she crossed the threshold into the old cathedral in Barcelona. Not the *Sagrada Família* but the Gothic *Catedral de la Santa Creu i Santa Eulàlia.* There was something alive about that cathedral too. The cloister was clustered with thirteen geese; one for every year that Santa Eulàlia lived. There were palm trees there too. Outside, there were beggars, tradesmen, and travellers selling head coverings, scarves, and silk, in and around the doorways. These high places also demand a covering. The mountain is not my god but I realise, whenever my ankles begin to strain, that I am treading on holier ground.

Christians don't usually worship mountains. But was I obsessed with this particular mountain we were heading to? Had I become a devotee or even, an idolater? God forbid! But the area around Pic des Spijeoles had become a sort of obsession. I read up on it and started studying the hill that shunned me. I found some old Cassini Maps, or 'Maps of the Academy', that were produced by four generations of one family. Numbers 75 and 76 (the areas where I would go) were drawn up by César-Francois between the years 1771 and1781. I wanted to employ these because they were the first French maps to use geodetic triangulation and they were, therefore, geneses of map-making.

I then zoomed in on the mountain itself. The first (recorded) ascent was by Henry Russell (1834-1909) and his guide on June 30, 1880. He was one of the first 'pyreneists', the phenomenon, which Louis le Bondidier notes in 1908, is only associated with the outsider:

> *In order to become a perfect pyreneist, it is almost compulsory to not have been born a Pyrenean. The local Pyrenean is immune to the pyreneist germ.*

After all, man has been bothering the mountain, and the area surrounding it, for a long time. The local Pyreneans we encountered on the hills were usually bergers or shepherds; hill dwellers and sheep-keepers combined in the old French word bergier. They are usually sitting on a ledge, mesmerised by their flocks, hypnotised by the cacophony of bells that jingle with every bite of turf. They seem to be immune to that desire, whatever it actually is, that drives mankind to forbidden places. Or so they say. The locals have always crossed at the easiest points or have sought refuge far away from the peaks. Then the outsiders came.

~

Mount Sinai

Moses was a foreigner when he entered the Sinai Peninsula. His father in law must have warned him as Zipporah's eyes dampened with fear and love:

'We do not go up there... It is Yahweh's place. Moses, the mountain is holy and none have returned from its slopes,' Jethro said, emerging from the smoke-filled tent.

'I must see Him,' said Moses, his eyes constantly drawn to the alpenglow wrought by the presence of Yahweh Himself. Moses married the shepherdess; he became a berger; the berger became a mountaineer; the mountaineer became the Red Sea prophet who eventually returned to the same slopes which had drawn him after Egypt.

Based on Exodus chapters two and three

~

'Mountain-top-experiences' – another phrase which goes beyond the religious lexicon – is a prominent phrase in 'experiential Christianity.' The top of the hills is what it's all about. David and Habakkuk used the same image of a chamois-like creature in their work. In Psalm 18, David imagines God re-fashioning his feet into that of a hind before setting him on a high place.

The prophet Habakkuk also finishes his prophecy with a God who enables him to have hinds' feet for high places. I used to imagine these men striding across rocks like mythical creatures. In Solomon's songs – the greatest love poem ever written – his lovesick bride gazes at the Jewish hills, longing for her beloved's return:

Make haste my beloved, and be thou like to a roe or to a young hart upon the mountains of spices.

Later, I found out that this ancient king was a type of Christ, and how early Christians would read or sing these songs as love ballads to their Saviour. I also realised that they were not talking about literal hills. Was it that Danish philosopher Søren Kierkegaard (1813-1855) that used a map metaphor in his writings? He emphasised that it is no good just sitting at home and reading a map, one has to go and experience that map (that's what I got from it anyway). He was using the metaphor in order to talk about the difference between head-knowledge religion (the spectator) and experienced religion (the pilgrim). True faith involves valleys, mist, hardship, leaps, river crossings, uphill battles, dangers, meadows, falls, terror, awe, and mountain-top experiences. But before every mountain-top are the valleys and the difficult climbs. Gazing at the map is not good enough. You've got to get going.

My father and I were nearing Lac d'O'ô. We knew we were getting close because over-enthusiastic Frenchmen, with binoculars around their necks, were telling us that we did not have far to go; as if we were on the verge of discovering the source of the Nile. One of them had the 'Oh, they're definitely-father-and-son' look written on his face. Dad does resemble me. We are both quite tall and both hypochondriacs. He is an economist, though, and his hair is very grey. It turned that colour around the time of my genesis. We both like books, fishing, and mountains. For years, he used to go up the hills on his own. We would say goodbye to him and he would come back a week later sunburnt and very healthy, or sunburnt and very sick. He'd always give us leftover sweets before spending another week recovering in bed after drinking bad water. There were other times when he would sit at the table and tell us about all the refuges, some French guy he walked with called Jacques, thunder and lightning, demonic rams, thirst, drinking out of puddles, sleeping in bus shelters, monasteries, eagles, ghosts in the clouds, strange rainbows, bridges, caves, paths and finally, all those peaks he'd conquered. To be fair, he tuned my mind and planted wonderful images there. There were times when he would take me for walks after supper. We live in a rural village and the pathways get very dark in the evenings. Dad would start fuelling my imagination like an engine-driver pouring coal into the steam train:

'There used to be elves in this area,' he'd say with gospel certainty.

'Elf?' I'd grab on to his coat.

'Yes… and dwarves… You see that tree?'

'What tree?'

'That tree! Look! Can you see him watching you!' I saw the creatures form as my imagination rolled on word-formed tracks like a Flying Scotsman. It was like peeping through the bushes and seeing the magic of C.S. Lewis' Dancing Lawn. One minute he'd say: 'Look an owl!' The next: 'a troll!' As I grew up I learnt to control my vision. But the swoop of a barn owl whilst putting the bins out still scares me. It'll be quite uncanny when I go grey as well. We'll look like twins. We smiled politely at the Frenchman and continued towards the lake.

A café stood in our way. What's worse, between us and the path, we observed a flock of colourful North Face tourists avidly positioning themselves for Facebook selfies. An overweight lady pushed me into the shallows of the lake as she passed me whilst her asthmatic son destroyed some flowers with a large stick shouting 'I'm Spiderman! I'm Spiderman!' He obviously hadn't read the sign which forbade the picking of rare flora and it hadn't clicked that Spiderman never carried a sword or stick. This was a bad beginning. Myself, I felt a bit like Quixote with my axe (which I'd only ever used once), rucksack, boots, and my staff. But, with my belly, I looked more like Sancho Panza.

The two of us stood on the edge hurriedly downing Fanta. I recently found an old photo of the lake taken quite close to where we were standing. Two characters stand out. The first is the man in the beret; I think he is some kind of guide leaning on his staff in fake contentment, waiting for these tourists to get some of their annual fresh air. The cascade looks like the doorway to Valhalla whilst the second character, a girl in the left hand corner, seems as if she wants to talk to us or escape from the stifling atmosphere of her walking party. She either doesn't belong in that photograph or she makes it a very good one. You can see the mountains watching. The people would be sitting somewhere else today because a cafe has been built on that spot. Even O'ô and its Valhalla gate has been changed forever. I didn't notice the waterfall. After grabbing another drink, we carried on towards Espingo.

Henri Tournier, 'Lac d'O'ô' (1858)

The path went on and on and on. Every bonjour silently turned into an au revoir as the people slowly disappeared. Usually they turn back after the first lake. You climb higher, the rocks get closer, and the cliff walls are intimately driven towards you as drops intensify on your right. Now and again, those Valhalla gateways wash over the path. They are not as spectacular when you are up close but they are refreshing when the sun is hot. Zigzags continue before you reach a gulley, notorious for being sun-blasted, making it seem like an eternal oven. Necessity brought us here, not pleasure. As you climb up the gulley, the ridge gets closer and closer, and eventually, buildings appear out of the blue.

It was Refuge d'Espingo. At first, it looks like bits of a Hornby railway station without the trains. Most refuges have a stony platform in front of their façades where climbers wait in the smoky cloud for a view. These are stations where novices fear the next day or where experts plan their difficult routes, drawing in the air, pointing with their rough fingers at gaps and gullies in the hill. Their fingers stretch out from the sleeves of well-worn goose down jackets unlike the novices, whose gear is far too clean. There are usually benches, a tap for drinking water, a dog, and the churning sound of an ancient generator making up for missing trains.

The mountain came into view. It looked different the second time. The place where I had fallen was no longer white but a dull grey. The snow was gone and the long silk-like ridge flowed from the cliff in a wave of boulders. I dreaded the morning. I must have looked like an old man, tattered, upon my stick. Dad looked young. He was almost waiting for the cue to carry on but the impending darkness said no and drove him obediently inside. We never cease from exploration. And the end of our exploring is arriving back where we started. Whenever Dad comes to the hills, he is young again. The slow low notes of darkness finally led me into the warmth as well. Outside, everything was formless.

That evening, we sat in a dim, cosy dining room. The tables were set out like a scriptorium. Medieval bowls and jugs of wine looked as if they'd just been transported from Cana where *Kixmi* had first shown who He really was.[4] On our table there was an English couple. One looked like a monk, the other a nun, and both had ginger hair. He was shaking and she was staring at another climber at the end of the table. I had seen this pair walking up to the refuge like *burro* (donkeys) with big packs on their backs. He was her master, and she was his. Their faces reflected their mood and their mood never seemed to change. Their braying continued throughout the evening and I wondered whether their woolly hats had anything to hide. Next to them was Dad with his two big hands, fidgeting on the table. The food was very basic: mutton

4 *Kixmi* – what the Basques first called Christ.

stew, dried bread and mushy apple for afters. This was a meal that would repeat itself in many of the refuges. We had obviously picked the wrong table. The donkeys went on and on whilst the other table sounded much more interesting. Seven Catalonian climbers were playing dominoes – their faces were animated and their gaze was full. So many things lingered in the corridors of their eyes.

There was a hustle outside and the faint sound of a dog barking. The donkeys fell silent and their heads turned to the door. A figure walked in from the dark. The dog drove him in, dripping, grunting, like an old dog himself. He had a big moustache and a tale-telling face containing a library of experience. He seemed to know the Catalans and he greeted them before sitting next to us. The bench made a noise and his fingers landed on the table like battered vessels coming into a harbour. They were big, like mine, but they were dirty, weary, and old. He cared for his face but the rest of his body seemed to be glued to his clothes which were stained and battle worn.

'*Vin*?' he asked the ginger woman, pointing at their ration. The woman looked at her husband who replied:

'This is ours I'm afraid.'

'Uh?' The stranger looked amazed.

'Ours… *Mon… vin… Mer-ci*!' in British staccato.

'I know it's yours! That is not polite!' The stranger shouted in a French lisp. At this point, my father gave him the jug near us, in a rush to diffuse the brewing tension. This became a seal of our friendship and a peace offering that was well worth making. From now on, we would be known as *'mes amis gallois'* (My Welsh friends).We thought it better not to reveal that Dad was actually English.

I christened him Hemingway because he looked like that photo of the author crouching down on his fishing boat. His eyes were the same colour as the sea, cheerful and undefeated by a hard day's walk. He ate his food in a particular way. His eyes would be fixed before him as if he were staring at a painting in a gallery or listening to Erik Satie playing a gymnopédie. As he ate his mutton stew I saw his jolly face descend into misery. The reason for this despondency was the large quantity of bone swimming in his portion. What occurred next was worth witnessing, and I was pleased to be sitting nearby. He shouted. He shuffled. He waved a soggy piece of mutton around in the sky like a pagan who had just extracted a cow's heart. There was no blood, but we were being sprinkled with drops of mutton juice whilst the grumpy hostel wardens (which are called *guardians* in mountain-lingo) stood puzzled. Hemingway argued that the food was, and I quote, *'merde'*, and for the price he was paying we should have better. After receiving an extra portion of meat he re-commenced his meal. His moustache moved up and down, up and down for a while. He ate and drank in a way that is only seen in someone who has been on his own for a very long time. He returned to the art gallery of his mind.

Hemingway came from Alsace. His father was a German soldier during the war and his mother was a French villager. He was a border man; from a place of fuzzy nationalities where identity leaves a trail of question marks linking together and building criss-cross borders inside people. Perhaps that is why he was drawn to the Pyrenees. This is a real border after all. People don't decide this one. God did. God decided that a wall of stone would separate two beautiful countries – a fixed wall which people adjusted to rather than re-drew. My father says he remembers walking in the Pyrenees for the first time as a young man. He reached the border and as soon as he passed into Iberia, a pair of guards stopped him. They were wearing those funny tricorn hats with capes over one shoulder. Their moustaches looked out of date and the men were almost glad to see another human. They checked his passport and let him go on. They seemed very small against the backdrop of the great Pyrenean wall. There are no soldiers now except for the mountains, caped with snow, peaked with rugged hats whilst shouting their stormy commands with thunder and avalanche.

Border-crossing is a daily occurrence in the Pyrenees. You can cross from France to Spain quite easily. But there are other lands there as well. Andorra is official but the Basques, the Occitans and the Catalans also demand a name. There are others who simply call the Pyrenees home. And because of that, they have a worthy stake in this natural inheritance. The borders are marked by solitary stones or by little yellow signs that give you a distance to the next lake, refuge, or town. Cols, passes, plains, chimneys and roads are all borders. Even peaks are sometimes situated on these invisible lines.

The hills border other realms too. If angels come then this is where they walk. Each place is unfamiliar, some 'thing' other always feeling near. Man's days are as grass; so many have plodded up the passes and destroyed the turf with their knees, shepherds have shinned the heights and followed the sheep before discovering forests of burning bushes. When they finally reach the top, they are driven mad, or they die, or poetry is born. God dwells in the mountains; there was the Shekinah on Sinai; then the angel on Moriah; He came as fire on Carmel before Calvary bore His incarnated stamp. Mountains are holy because they rise above the plain, above humanity itself, setting its two or three dwellers apart from the other disciples in the valley. One eremite, called Placidus a Spescha, regularly climbed an Alp near his Swiss monastery in order to spend the night closer to God. He must have been cold in his cowl! In Tibet, he would not have been able to sleep on Kailas. It is so holy that it is forbidden to climb it. Other mountains mean different things. Mount Ararat was humanity's second chance when Noah bagged its peak in an unconventional way. The ark rested on the cairns, the rainbow appeared as the waters died down. But now Ararat marks a lost Armenia – a hushed-up genocide, a border re-drawn, and a stolen mountain.

Each hill is a small window on eternity. R.S. Thomas said that Wales had so many jewels to gather, but with the eye only. The Welsh can grow rich by looking but he warned that those who crowd a small window dirty it with their breathing. Whilst breathing on the window, they built cafés on the peaks and showered the hills with green turbines hoping that they were camouflaged enough. Viewpoints were barricaded for the sake of health and safety and before long the peaks were no longer set apart from the valley below. Other mountains were burdened with Tower of Babel paths, allowing everybody to climb up and experience the inexhaustible views. I can almost hear the hills groaning when joggers bombard their shoulders with the pitter-patter of trainers. The poet-priest in the red tie believed that this wealth was only for the chosen few. Whoever these people are may they find their Eldorado in the Pyrenees. Or maybe we should take the Kailas approach.

Time stops. One day is as a thousand and all the

events along your walk seem to fuse together into a long panoramic photograph. The mountains represent antiquity and symbolise stability. The routes change. Track turns to single lane. Single turns to double. Double evolves into road. Barriers, signposts, wells and benches are erected. Dwellings come and go. Animals are wiped out and humans move along like nomads in rocky deserts. Even the glaciers melt and the surface of the hills gains wrinkles, loses grass, develops spots and shrivels up like skin. But the mountain has always been there. We weren't there at the beginning. And because of that we can never expect or anticipate the mountains' end.

Hemingway finished his meal. We talked with him for a while about his past and tried to extract his story from him. His fingers moved like those little boats in a Battleships game. He was a social worker and was spending the aftermath of his divorce trekking the Pyrenees. His eyes were talking before he even opened his mouth to blurt out:

'My wife was stifling; she was really, really bad!'

'I understand—' I wasn't sure how to answer his statement.

'I don't think you do... Listen *amis*, a good wife is one in a million. My advice to you is: don't hurry. Climb peaks and do not expect good marriage. In fact, it is likely that you have bad marriage,' he abruptly paused before asking, 'what is your mother like?'

By this time my father had gone out to make a phone call. He often does that; he comes and goes even when people are trying to talk to him. I looked around and the Catalans were smoking indoors right underneath the forbidding symbol saying *Défense de Fumer* which they, as did I, re-fashioned to say 'defend your smokes'. The English monk and nun had gone to bed and I was left alone with Hemingway.

'My mother is… very short,' I don't know why I said it. I tend to say the first thing that comes to my mind.

'Ha! Short, you say? That's okay. Does she keep a good house?'

'Yes, she is a very good mother and I believe she is a very good wife.'

'Ha! Does she cook?' He kept saying 'ha', which I think was a good thing.

'Yes,' I answered.

'That is a good house!' He grabbed my shoulder and shook it like a captain congratulating one of his sailors.

My father re-emerged, complaining about the lack of signal. Hemingway said that he liked us, and as a mark of his love, he bought us some 'apple wine' which looked like a kind of cider. I didn't have the heart to tell him that I was teetotal – that's an anathema in France anyway. The photograph of a cousin drained and beaten by the bottle had left an impression on me. Looking at his photograph was a bit of a Dorian experience; there was a resemblance which needed to be eradicated, avoided, and hidden in the attic. Hemingway grinned as he gave us a bottle each. I looked at the bottle and decided to drink it to be courteous. I felt ashamed but his face consoled me. This was a Ghost-of-Christmas-Present character and his conversation was full of 'Come in and know me better, man', so much so, that I started adding holly, mistletoe, red berries, ivy, turkeys, geese, game, poultry, oysters, pies, puddings, fruit and punch into the scriptorium refuge. There was a ruddy glow that was always on the brink of vanishing. But for now, the room was glowing.

He coughed very loudly before rolling a cigarette. He continued:

'You see… this is a bad house… E-s-p-i-n-g-o,' emphasising each letter before

shouting: 'more like E-s-shshsh-i-t-s-o! I never tasted such bad food! It is very, very important to keep a good house!'

The imaginary food vanished instantly. Hemingway carried on for a while before the conversation turned to his next victims, the English hillwalkers:

'You saw that couple?' he turned his head to the direction of the dormitory.

'Yes, why?'

'They are… what you call… winebibbers, as you British say.'

For a moment I wondered how he'd acquired that

word. I had only heard it in the Bible.

'Winebibbers?'

'Yes, winebibbers! I say… that woman keeps a bad house and that man is definitely an alcoholic! He has the shakes… I don't like English.'

I looked at my father. Hemingway continued as he smoked:

'What is the point of the Queen? She is… what do you call it… *tyran*… tyrant. The English bow down to her as if she is god. *Mon Dieu*! This is idolatry if you ask me and one more thing, we French would have her head for sure.'

He started humming *La Marseillaise*. He winked at us as he left the table.

Refuge d'Espingo is actually not that bad. The warden has been there since my father was a young man and they've aged together. My father reckons that in all the years that he has visited the place, the warden has spoken two or three sentences to him. One of those was condemnation after I fell, for taking me up the mountain without crampons. It's also a good place because it has toilet paper. Most refuges do not. If you ever go to a refuge in the Pyrenees, be sure to take some toilet paper with you. There's nothing more disheartening than arriving and seeing a dark, stinking hole with flies buzzing around it. There is usually no toilet except for a squatting platform, and then to cap it all, no paper. It's the same feeling that someone must have felt when staring into an empty sarcophagus after walking through a pyramid. Up in the mountains paper is gold and from that moment, if away hiking, I always carried a spare roll.

One year I was staying in Refuge Le Soula in the Valleé de Louron. There was an urgent need to use the toilet because I had drunk bad water on the hill that day. I entered the stinking area and was horrified when I saw the bare toilet roll holder. I felt discouraged and worried. All I had was a copy of Zafon's latest book in the *Shadow of the Wind* series. Chapter 1 was sacrificed for a good cause. I don't know why they don't have proper toilets in France. My dad lost his phone down the hole once. For future reference, always zip your pockets up and if you don't have roll, then receipts, pages from a book, or even restaurant napkins always come in handy.

Night comes quickly in the Pyrenees, far quicker than it does in cities. Lights don't orange up the sky and the moon only paints the hillsides grey and white. Nights can become bright days when your imagination is active. Days can become night-like when tiredness or schedules rob you of the surrounding glory. But at twilight, you are still again. There is time to look around before the stars draw your gaze upward.

The dining room was nearly empty. The click, click,

of moving chess pieces was in one corner whilst Dad was stroking his eyebrows in another. This was one of Dad's things. He spent his evenings planning the route and memorising the maps. His memory is good when it comes to places, books, and routes. But he's hopeless with faces. Dad is very English and I am very Welsh. I am a fount of feeling: my cup always overflows. Dad is more reserved. I turned towards the little, old-fashioned window and saw a glowing light pulsating in the mist. Hemingway was standing outside. Our friend was smoking and staring up the valley at a distant point. He was a big owl in the moonlight, his head moving side to side, surveying the area like a lord. Now and again his fingers twitched before he coughed and ended the ritual by spitting on the floor. He returned like Moses. His face was glowing and I knew that he was going to say something.

'Ha! *Mes amis gallois*!' We both stopped doing nothing and looked towards him. 'It is time for bedtime story, no?' We both smiled. 'I will tell you about my first peak.'

'In the Pyrenees?' Dad asked,

'*Oui.*'

This was his first story about his first day on the mountain. In a strange way, we all share these genesis moments. It went something like this.

~

The Tale of Hemingway and the Virgin Mary

Antziñan, in the old days, Hemingway began his mountaineering as a boy scout.[5] One weekend, his troop travelled down to the Pyrenees to help the local church with some repair work. This would involve working on the church building itself but it also meant that the boys would repair the various shrines, summit crosses and graveyards in the vicinity. They were staying in a church hall somewhere in the Basque country.

Early one morning, Hemingway was suddenly woken up by the priest, who was a grotesque sight. The priest seemed to be a continuation of Hemingway's nightmares. One of their guides was a Basque storyteller and he had waxed eloquently on witches, demons, and shooting stars into the early hours. His stories took young Hemingway to the caves of Amboto and Mount Txindoki where beautiful, evil women spent their time designing curses in cahoots with the Prince of Darkness.[6] One story – 'A Mother's Curse' – invaded his mind. In the cavern of Amboto, a certain woman spent hours and hours spinning and spinning but never making thread.[7]

---

5 Antziñan – 'In the old days…' Tis is how some of the old Basque stories begin. All further references to the stories and legends are based on Luis de Barandiaran Irizar (ed.), *A View from the Witch's Cave: Folktales of the Pyrenees* (Reno & Las Vegas: University of Nevada Press, 1991).

6 These are various caves in the Pyrenees. Like Taenarum, they are associated with the Underworld.

7 The legend 'A Mother's Curse'. recorded by José de Azcárate, Marin, in 1934.

She had no clothes. The only garb she wore was her long blonde hair which embraced her youthful body like a shawl. He watched her. At midnight, she left her cavern and joined her sisters in the stream of sparks. His dream continued with the woman spitting out the host (the bread/body of Christ) during Mass, treading on her rosaries during confession before being carried away by Lucifer to Amboto. Lucifer was about to take Hemingway too before he was woken up by the priest's cold hand slapping him on his cheek.

The dream disturbed him. The priest disturbed him. The morning definitely disturbed him because it was so cold. As a punishment for not waking up sooner, the priest handed him a rather large object that he would carry up the hill. He couldn't see what it was. The boys formed a line behind the babbling priest. Some carried tools, others carried picnics, one had a bugle, and a couple of others were in charge of a *burro* that bore the pieces of another Calvary that would be erected on the summit.

The priest looked like a Cheshire cat. It was dark but Hemingway remembers his teeth which were unnaturally white, especially as they emerged from a mouth of the crow-like man. They started walking up the dewy bank. Their feet became wet and cold within five minutes and their faces told the tale of an undevout pilgrimage. The priest's lantern swung to and fro, like a giant censer, baptising them with welcomed light.

Hemingway decided that if he couldn't see what he was carrying he would smell it and feel it instead. It smelt of paint. It felt smooth. He could make out some features along its side. The top was round and he was sure that he could feel a nose-like feature. It was very heavy. About halfway up the mountain, Hemingway dropped his package and heard a crack. He picked it up, quickly feeling it for any damage. Whatever that nose-like feature had been it was now no more and he suddenly felt sick.

The light came. It was good and bad. The mountain looked big and they were all so small. Hemingway took a peek at his package, determined to investigate the damage. He untied the rope and looked in.

The first thing he saw was an eye which nearly shook the living daylights out of him. Then he saw a face and the blue and white indicated that he had been carrying the Virgin Mary herself (well, a statue of her). For some reason, her face looked angrily at him and he soon realised why. Her nose had completely disappeared and the white spot in the middle of her face had an awful effect on the artwork. She looked more Sphinx than Holy Mother. That soft, white, French face was grimacing. He couldn't stop giggling. He concluded that noses were a vital aspect of one's face. Not necessarily for smell-sake (he concluded that even if one lost a nose there would still be a hole for the smells to enter) but for beauty's sake! Mary looked terrible without her nose. She looked angry and most unpleasant.

The rest of the story is quite tragic. The priest heard him chuckling. He walked over and the priest nearly experienced a seizure when he saw her face. Hemingway was beaten by the crow and his parents had to pay for a new nose. Nevertheless, the boys managed to replace the cross on the summit and they enjoyed a picnic afterwards, sharing some of their food with the faithful *burro*.

The procession came down the hill. The crow was angry. The *burro* felt young again. The boys found it all amusing having to carry Mary safely on her way. This time, another boy was roped in to grab her feet. Thankfully, she descended safely.

Based on a story told by Hemingway to the author

~

That was Hemingway's first peak and he laughed as he told us the story. He said that every time he went up to those high places in the Basque Country he would see her face, angrily looking at him again. He also noted that he always looks for her nose, which is probably still hiding somewhere on the mountainside.

'*Mes amis*, look out for Mary's nose will you! One day, I can imagine some English coming across it. Haha, what a thought, no?'

'What happened to the priest?' Dad asked.

'I don't know. He was a very nasty man. Never trust a priest especially a priest that hits his donkey!'

Dad was nodding and I nodded too. Hemingway laughed before deciding that another cigarette was needed. He grinned at us both before saying bonne nuit and making the sign of the cross above us like an old bishop.

Going to bed is always an interesting experience in refuges. Usually, the lack of space means that there is only one long bunk bed. It can sometimes be three-storied and your ankles are in danger if you sleepwalk. You are given a flat pillow unwashed since the days of Charlemagne, a blanket fit for Rob Roy, and a mattress which smells a little too sweet. The snoring is unbearable and a pair of earplugs is recommended. That night, as I entered the sleeping area, the English couple were perched like a pair of characters from *Pilgrim's Progress* reading their Kindles in their own sleeping bags and resting on their own feather pillows that they had carried all the way. The blankets did make you itch and my dreams were full of fleas and feet. These are either your own feet which are always sore, or the imaginings of all the other sore feet that have slept where your feet do.

Hemingway had disappeared. I didn't know where he'd gone. There were a few German whispers and then a bang. He entered, giggling like a little boy. All I could see was a bouncing moustache, his eyes and his ears. He jumped up and prepared his bed right next to me. For some reason he looked as if he had no body. The light in the window illuminated his face, and only his face. This was funny in itself. His moustache was always moving as he giggled and snorted and his eyes glistened by the wedge of lunar in his orbs. We both looked at one another and laughed. Somebody had broken wind. Dad was snoring.

I half expected that morning would never come and the company was so good that I didn't mind. Our mutton meal was swapped with mirth and this strange experience of giggling in the night warmed our spirits. The wind howled outside. The corrugated roof rattled. It didn't matter. Hemingway was the greatest host. This wasn't even his house but it was glowing in the darkness. I almost spoke Welsh to him. It was a strange situation when you think about it. I was lying in bed next to a man that looked like Ernest Hemingway. Next to him were two Germans. Next to me was my father. Underneath us, the English pilgrims were reading and sighing while the dog praised God outside with his growl and cry. We could have been on Noah's ark itself. The storm was bad outside and we were inside like pairs of survivors – animals in our pens. It was like being in that closed-up cave on Grassholm for eighty years with the talking head. Have you heard about

Bendigeidfran, the giant king from Welsh mythology? After being defeated in Ireland, seven men survived and transported Bendigeidfran's head wherever they went. It is said that at Gwales (Grassholm) they lived eighty years without perceiving the passing of time in a cave where the head was very much alive and a 'great host.' Eventually, one of them opens the door of the cave and all the joy and gladness is suddenly replaced with sorrow. If someone had opened our door it would have all been over and my story ruined. But that night, after Hemingway told of his 'virgin' peak, I realised that all our stories are very similar. I started thinking about the grand narrative, the same record machine that plays these different records. Perhaps the machine is played by that listener; he lifts the arm with his big hand and when the needle hits the record, music begins. This is the moment when finger meets finger and we live.

At around 6.30 a.m. our head-torches were lit. Cycloptic eyes started moving in the dark. There were groans. The odd snore accompanied by the sound of some inquirer looking out to see if the waters had died down. I looked out as well. I saw a dog barking before flying up the hill like a dove with an olive branch in his mouth. He returned with the stick and his master threw it again. In the distance, I could see the old mountain waiting for us. For a moment I remembered lying on its slope, totally in its mercy, incanting silent words, prayers and babbling about green fields. The smell of feet brought me back to the refuge. I've always had a sensitive nose and the smells in these places are always overwhelming. A quick burst of spray made incense in the dark small space. Dad was already wandering around like Noah. I felt like a miner. Hemingway was old again. The talking head had finally become silent and he lay there like a sleeping lord. Would he awake again, I wondered? We carried on, not knowing whether we would ever see this man again.

The evening and the morning were the first day.

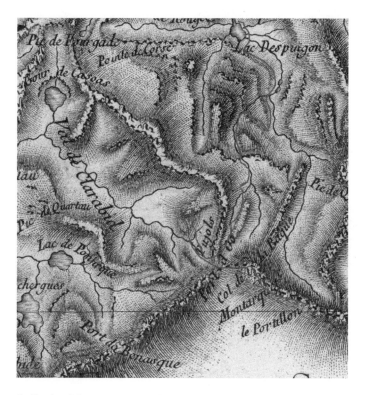

Spijeoles Map

2

Plòu, plòu ramalhaud,
Las vachas baten los buòus,
Dins los prats los parpalhòus
E los 'limaçs leven lu còu.

Raining, raining tadpoles,
The cows are beating the oxen,
In the fields those butterflies
And slugs are raising their heads.

Occitan Poem

There are times when sky and earth war against one another. That great division between high and low is suddenly bridged by water. We are included in this cycle. You cannot see the mountains but you know that the water is falling. In the fields, the butterflies raise their heads. Their antennae move as our heads gaze upward. These flowers fly and their dye-dusty wings flap before their colours are washed away.

Cairn on Pointe Muga Nord

Paths in the Pyrenees are usually marked by cairns. These little pyramids are made up of individual stones laid on top of one another one-by-one. A cairn may indicate the peak of a mountain or a col. But the smaller cairns usually mark out a route. When appearing near to one another, you follow the path by going from cairn to cairn. At other times they are scattered across the hillside and your eyes strain as you try and differentiate between what is man-made and what is simply a natural coincidence.

There are many paths but most of them turn out

to be sheep tracks. Transhumance still occurs in the Pyrenees. The people move their animals in their quest for better pasture. The noise of an approaching someone usually bleats before coming fully into view. As you walk behind a flock, it feels as if the mountains move in their sleep. These rocky somnambulists feed on the high air. The moisture tricks your eyes and the hills start following you like behemoth grazers. In Wales, we used to have places known as *hafodydd* which were summer residences for the farming families when staying high up. The *hafod* can still be seen in the Pyrenees. Little stone cabins dotted on the hillsides, and, if you peer through the windows, you can see the marks of life – a stove, firewood and blankets – the basic needs are met. The shepherds move uphill in May or June and then return in September. In Wales, the quadbike has taken over. The hills are still and the sheep are all alone in the bracken.

In some stone cabins, the *bergers* make *brebis*. This is a sheep's cheese made on the hillside. One year, we came across what looked like a traveller's camp on the shoulder of the mountain. We heard barking and we armed ourselves with stick and axe. Relief followed when the shepherd called his dog away, waving at us and bidding us to pass in peace. Behind him, his family were eating their lunch. In that *hafod* I saw the cheese-making implements and the wind-carved face of the farmer. Next to him were his children; they were laughing.

A Pyrenean Hafod

As you follow the cairns, you will notice that a certain animal enjoys sunbathing near the path. Alpine marmots (*Marmota marmot*) are rodent-like creatures that would prosper in any children's cartoon. In Switzerland, monuments are built for them because they are considered lucky. They became extinct in the Pyrenees because marmot fat was used as a cure for rheumatism whilst others were hunted for fur. However, they were successfully re-introduced in 1948 and they now run like little beavers across the rocky playground. Their eagle-like screech sounds out as they stand up like well-behaved, overweight meerkats. I like the *Marmota*. My father showed me a trick once which explained why they were nearly wiped out. We came across one of these furry friends and he held his stick up high, swaying it to and fro. This odd ritual became stranger as he walked closer and closer to the creature. *Marmota marmota* seemed mesmerised, religiously focussing on the tip of the stick. My father got so close that he could easily have grabbed him, and for a moment, man stared marmot in the face and they were friends. He then moved the stick and *Marmota* disappeared. When walking in the hills, you usually meet them once or twice a day unlike the chamois that are aloof and much higher up.

The ding-a-ling of the cowbells makes the lower hills as holy as the high places. The cows manage to make a mess but they provide music for the sleeping folds and crags. The paths are sometimes very good. The Grand Randonnée (GR) or Haute Randonnée Pyrénéenne (HRP), are long-distance footpaths. We sometimes used the HRP, the GR10 and GR11. The GR is marked by red and white paint which, if followed correctly, will take you the whole length of the Pyrenees. These pathways criss-cross through the valleys and they are a welcome change from following the unreliable cairns. Hemingway was following the GR10 which would take him from sea to sea. We were walking a circuit which sometimes crossed over the different GRs. Dad prefers this because you're not stuck with ramblers all day. When you go off-route you see better things and the people are usually more interesting. Plus, it allows my father to use his maps properly rather than the easier method of following the marks.

As I passed the red and white marks, I kept thinking

about Passover.[8] A long time ago, the Jews painted their doorframes with lamb's blood before death passed them by. Screams and horrors were heard throughout Egypt but the Jews were safe because of the blood. This was a long night for the Jews and it would be the first of many. In a way, these red marks saved us too on many occasions, especially when we were walking in the mist. The red and white cross shows that there is a danger ahead whilst the arrows point you in the right direction. I have often wondered who actually paints these signs. I imagined swallow-like angels landing on the paths. One of them carefully carried a pot of paint, the other one illuminated the rocks before the next walker passed by.

Our destination was not a holy mountain. We knew that our car was the end of the journey. We would do a couple of peaks, meet incredible people but there was no particular goal. Hemingway was heading towards the Atlantic and I started to wonder whether the water had some kind of answer for him. The Catalans, who we'd seen the night before, were heading towards Aneto, the highest mountain in the Pyrenees at 3,404m. They were determined travellers following in the footsteps of the great traveller, Louis Ramond de Carbonnières who described Aneto as having 'needles of ice' in 1787. Not much has changed except that there is less ice which seems to be disappearing with the glaciers.

8 For an account of the first Passover, see Exodus 12.

My father and I were simply passing through; we sojourners in this big church, where God was making himself felt.

After leaving d'Espingo, it was time to ascend Pic des Spijeoles for the second time. This was the moment that I had been dreading and I had lost count of how many times I had re-climbed those hundred yards in my sleep.

'Do you think it'll be alright?'

'You what?'

'Do you think it'll be okay this time? The hill, you know?'

'Oh, should be. There's no snow.'

Walking dumbs your fear. That morning, the fire salamanders (*Salamandra salamandra*) followed us on the damp path. Their yellow and black skin clashed with the green of the valley floor whilst their black boots moved in sync with my bigger brown boots. According to Breton legend, you must never say the salamander's real name because if he hears you, he'll kill you with his deadly abracadabra. So, instead of talking, we walked together awhile in perfect silence.

The mountain grew as we approached it. I was walking slowly because one of the salamanders persistently followed me. Before turning up the first climb, the path passes some font-like lakes. A solitary fly fisherman, accompanied by his sheepdog, stood on the shore. The salamander stopped as soon as he saw the dog. Like a wizard's wand, the fisherman's line swirled in the air before landing peacefully on the glassy lake. His whipping motion looked as if he was trying to grab the other side. Strike. Fail. Strike. Fail: the distress on his face intensifying with every cast. He started talking to himself. '*Mon Dieu... Allons... Mon Dieu... S'il vous plait.*' Fishermen are as religious as climbers. Fishermen talk to the water and fear its power over both themselves and the fish. There is nothing for a long time. They cry to the sea and to the lakes. Still nothing. They add more bait, the bloodier the better. Nothing. Then, suddenly, there is a stirring. A silver shine disturbs the deep and an object appears like a miracle. Answered prayer is exchanged with more blood. They smack the fish's head and thank their god by dyeing the water red.

~

The Story of the Depressed Fishermen

'I go a-fishing', one of them said, taking off his tunic and pushing the boat into the blue.

'Shall we go?' The one called Didymus looked at the others. The others shrugged before following him into the boat.

The night rolled on and they caught nothing. They were hungry, tired, and sore. The waves made the water look like a small mountain range whilst the fishermen looked like giants mining the mountains for silver. Eventually, their leader threw the knife on the deck and let his face fall into the palms of his hands.

'Who's that, waving at us?' Ioan said, staring at a lonely figure on the beach. He pulled the ropes from the boat floor and untangled some of the knots.

'You caught anything?' The figure shouted. He was standing next to a bivouac of sea wood. A small string of smoke signaled his position on the sand.

At first, none of them answered. Then Peter, their leader, suddenly let out a great big 'No!'

'Cast your nets on the other side!' the stranger shouted.

There was a silence. But they listened nonetheless. Fishermen are always on that ridge between faith and doubt. The men looked down into the deep blue valleys below the boat. There was nothing. Suddenly, there was a stirring. Blue became silver as eyes upon eyes and eyes came up from the deep. They trembled.

'It's Rabbi.' Peter covered his nakedness and jumped into the sea. He swam like the fish but the fish were no longer on his mind.

Based on the account in John 21

～

After the lake, the path turned up towards the ridge. The snow was gone this time and the slope seemed easier. I paid homage to the place where I fell. I imagined myself in the snow and tried to find the exact spot. A sense of closure descended upon me as I ascended beyond the fall point. I could now go further and proceed upwards into the unknown as if this were the first time. I excitedly proceeded. I think Arthur Ransome once said that all the best charts and maps have an 'Unexplored' area written on them. Even though men have clambered up these places, they felt unexplored to me. I felt like the first man.

Pic des Spijeoles

We scrambled to the top. I was expectant. Like Samuel, I started hearing my name whispered in the breeze. Samuel was an Old Testament prophet who, when sleeping in the sanctuary as a youth, heard the voice of God calling him three times. Was the wind playing tricks with me? I had to say something; 'Yes, Dad?'

'I didn't say anything,' it was like being in Shiloh.

'Nathan,'

'Yes Dad?

'I didn't say anything,' he would answer again with that half giggle people give when they think you're going mad. I wanted to hear my name a third time. Would there be a smoky bush or even just the charcoal remains of a burnt-out tree around the corner? Nothing.

The peak was getting nearer. I knew it because the temperature was dropping and we were rapidly running out of ground. One minute you're on all fours and then you suddenly grab air and the panorama strikes you: a sea of hills and a silence which is only disturbed by the sound of your own eerie footsteps. The top of the hill had a cairn on it. We crawled towards it and sat down.

'Look,' I called Dad over.

At 3065m, underneath a couple of small stones, we unearthed a little tin box which looked as if it had fallen under Zeus's wrath a couple of times. I opened the box and pulled out a little notebook in a plastic poly-pocket. The pages were yellowed with age but the writing was legible. I read a list of names from all over the world. We signed our names, emphasised Pays de Galles, and conjured up the notion that I was the first Welshman to tread that high place before shoving the little book back into its rusty container. The light was rapidly changing. Refuge d'Espingo had long since disappeared beneath us and we were now privy to the shadows in the sky.

In the 1600s, Jacob Scheuchzer drew up a compendium of dragons that supposedly existed in the Alps. The Franciscan writer Salimbene of Parma recounted how Peter of Aragorn climbed to the summit of a mountain where he was met by a '*draco horribilis*' (dreadful dragon) with huge wings that blocked out the sun. In the Pyrenees, when birds send silhouettes on the rocks, the old folk believed them to be witches rather than '*draco horribilis*'. Here, the shadows are usually formed by vultures. When the sun suddenly disappears and you hear the loud swish of the passing bird, you will understand why the distinction between witch and vulture is sometimes tricky. In Amboto, a beautiful lady could be seen every day flying towards Kutzebarri. The Basques believed that as the witches crossed the heavens, they would comb their long hair with exquisite, magical combs making a unique 'pir-pir' sound before turning into big birds.[9] The vultures on Spijeoles were beginning to fly lower. This meant

9 See legend 'The Theft of the Comb'. Recorded by José Aramburuzabal, from Escoriaza, in 1935.

that a storm was approaching although our next destination, the Refuge du Portillon, was still quite a long way away.

My father's face turned whiter. He set it like a flint towards our destination. Were we being punished for straying off the path? Perhaps it was a sin to come so high. None of the peak paths were marked with those whites and reds. Perhaps the angels were protecting us or maybe they wanted us to stay in the valley below. There are some days when every mountain feels as forbidden as Kailas. Birds occur magically as if there is a portal somewhere to higher places. Personally, I felt like a trespasser. In my head, there were two types of climber. My father belonged to the first group. Those who have experienced the very high places are never the same as the rest of us, the second group, who still feel unworthy when treading the holy places. That's how it feels. If you do go up, then a storm will get you.

The clouds were adorning the dark blue mountain like the beard of an angry old man. My father told me about the first Pyrenean storm that he'd experienced when he hid in the rock for forty-five minutes because the lightning was hitting the earth near him; he saw the bolts running down the hill like quicksilver. The grumbling noises developed into musketry. I looked back at my father. He wasn't blinking at all. He had stopped talking a while ago. All he'd said that afternoon was 'Just get down, stop tawking' in pure cockney.

Eventually we were running. I kept looking behind at our grand pursuer. That's what happens when you stray or stay too long on any path – time creeps up, and the finger of God seeks you out for an encounter. If it can't hit a rock, it'll hit you.

The wild flowers faded and the grass became still as the soil prepared itself for war. The mountain watched on, strong and sturdy, as the air began its assault on the ground. The boom, boom, was in the distance. The war drums were beginning whilst distant skirmishes were audible in the other valleys. The clouds looked like white-crested foam on the sea as the boom, boom, continued and the storm descended. There was no shelter and the rain was about to be released. Somewhere behind all the cloud, the sun was a knot of fire, struggling to be seen. Was this nature or was it the Lady of Aralar?

~

The Legend of the Lady of Aralar

In Ugarte, there is a cave called Azari-zulo where the Lady of Aralar lays down her head after travelling a long way. According to legend, she usually lives in the caves of Aralar, Aizkorri and Burumendi. During the nights, when she moves from one cave to another, there is tremendous thunder and lightning. The

Pyrenees have storms most days; therefore, she is on the move every day. In older times, two Christian men laden with relics and other holy items sought after the witch in order to prove her existence. They came to the cave. The storm had not started so they knew she was still inside. They entered and saw the most beautiful woman combing her hair. Between her and the men there were two gold candelabras like the ones in Versailles. Her hair was golden and the yellow light from the candles made it shimmer in the darkness of the cave. As soon as she realised that there were others present, she stopped combing and hid in the deepest part of the cave, leaving the candelabras unguarded. The men saw their chance and stole these objects before returning home, satisfied that they had seen the witch. As soon as they placed the candelabras on their kitchen tables something magical happened. The objects changed colour and the candleholders melted in a moment before re-moulding themselves into six toads. They hopped out of the windows and disappeared into the darkness.

Based on the legend 'The Lady of Aralar'.
Recorded by J. Arandia, from Amézqueta, in 1931

~

We were nearing Portillon as the Lady of Aralar stepped out from her cave. We ran down with a boiled sweet in one cheek each because we were utterly exhausted. There was a mountain in our way. I thought about the words of Jesus when he said that even faith as small as a grain of mustard seed could remove this mountain. I prayed. But like the prayers of Nicholas and Natasha Rostov, it was that kind of childish prayer that wanted to make sugar out of snow. I asked for safety instead. We crossed a plateau just beyond a mountain called Tusse de Montarque and started our descent towards the red dot on the map signifying another refuge. We were still in France but it felt like no-man's land. On the flat bits there were remnants of older storms where rocks had cracked or fallen. Glaciers had melted and left big, giant boulders in the most random places. We entered a rocky maze. It started to rain and the rock was getting slippery. We crossed the refuge threshold before a loud crack announced the battle born.

The refuge was smaller than the last one. It still felt like being on a boat. I suppose it's because it is always so wet outside. I looked around. Black and white photographs, a stove, monastery tables, benches, and dried plants from the hills. The central room usually has a bookcase. Bill Bryson, some modern French authors which I didn't recognise, Zola, Dickens, *The Hobbit*, the adventures of some overweight Marmot and *Fifty Shades of Grey*. The books are as random as the people that stay there. There's always a Bible and a *Livre d'or*. The *Livre d'or* is placed on its own shelf like the *Guru Granth Sahib*. Every climber, sojourner, pilgrim and wanderer writes their names and the date of their stay. Blue ink, black ink, handwriting as varied as footprints left in snow, smudge marks, drunken scribbles and beautiful prose. I would look at the book later on.

Nobody talks to one another at first. Some sit down sipping their chocolat chaud. Others read maps. Some chat in their native tongues whilst most of the others stare out of the small windows. Next to the books there are some games. Scrabble is popular. So is Jenga. Mountaineers enjoy making words and building towers. My observations were disturbed when Dad burnt himself as he tried to peep inside the stove.

'Ah! Blasted hot!'

The rain came like this:

rain
rain   rain   rain
rain rain rain rain rain rain
This was not drizzle, but heavy droplets which hurt as they landed. We were running.
The sky was rent   in two by
  lightning and there was a tremendous BANG
                as we jumped
                            into the porch.

It was the closest thing in my head to World War II bombs. It makes you shake. You are exposed to such power, light, noise, and force. Your mind is stripped and every room, corridor, and hallway inside your head is illuminated. Dad was used to it. He was more concerned about his finger which had developed a blister from the burn.

~

Mount Horeb

Elijah was climbing Mount Horeb. It was a difficult climb and a storm had caught him on the cliffs. YAHWEH caused a great, strong wind to smite the mountain and rent the boulders nearby. But YAHWEH was not in the wind. Elijah was shaking. His fingers were cold as he wrapped his rough cloak around his freezing hair. Suddenly there was a great big BANG and the storm moved from the sky down to the earth. An earthquake ripped the ground like a rent veil. But YAHWEH was not in the earthquake. Out of the chasm, a great fire burnt and the mountain changed into a volcano. Streams of orange and black burnt the rock whilst the smoke started choking the prophet. But YAHWEH was not in the fire or the smoke. To his relief he saw a gap in the rock. Elijah hurried to the opening and hid in his mantle. Whilst lying down, he heard a still, small voice.

Based on an account recorded in 1 Kings 19

~

The storm went on for a while. I sat near a window, forgetting that our food was on its way.

'Have you ever seen a storm like this?' An American quizzed a calm German whilst everybody else gathered by the windows. Dad had now produced his big first aid bag and was painting his finger white with Savlon. He was making that face which told everyone near him to stay away; 'I-will-bite-if-you-try-and-communicate-with-me' was written all over him. I looked out of the window again. The lake behind the refuge was beginning to look like high-definition television as it reflected the colours above. This was a light show that verged on the supernatural. My head had already been filling up with legends and myths after reading a book of Pyrenean folktales. Greys became purples and yellows. The clouds were luminous that night and all this colour, sound, and imagination transported me back into an estrakinburu, a Basque story that tells of the announcement of the birth of Kixmi, or Christ.

~

A Tale of Announcement – Estrakinburu

Two thousand years ago, there were many dancers at Aralar. Imagine the darkness and a bonfire at its centre. The mountains are hidden but the people are naked. Their eyes are flaming wicks whilst their bodies are wax-like, soft and energetic, malleable shadows in the light: free and furious, the men and women enveloped together in uncontrollable frenzy. Hand in hand they dance their tarantella polka – shouting, laughing, whistling, and whining – to the beat of the   feet   on the   trodden   turf. There are no children. The older ones sit on the periphery; some are hiding whilst others watch without blinking.

One of the dancers suddenly stops. He points at a luminous cloud which slowly approaches from afar. They call for the *azti* (prophet).

'Father! Father!'

There is no response.

'Father! Father!'

An older man comes into the light. His eyes are white whilst the rest of his body seems swallowed by the night.

'What is that coming towards us from the East?' They ask him as they watch his eyes turn towards the direction of the cloud. Between the cumuli he sees the Incarnation.

'My children!' He shouts. 'Kixmi has been born and

our end is near. I no longer wish to live… I beg you to throw me over that cliff!'

The dancers are stunned. They take the druid's body and throw him over the cliff without any emotion. They hear a thud which is the last note in a screaming requiem which sounded as he fell. Other wise men, seers, astronomers, and knowing ones had seen what the azti had seen that evening. Some even worshipped and followed the stars to Bethlehem. But this one would not. The *azti* realised that this omen heralded the end of Aralar's dance and he could not accept it. His naked body lay broken at the bottom of the cliff until the vultures came and finished off his grand disappearance. The luminous cloud continued to approach. The pagans scattered, fleeing to the rocks, higher and higher before realising that the light was getting closer and closer. One large group arrived at a beech tree grove in Arraztaran. The trees were brown and their leaves fell in a grand swoosh which sped up the seasons in a single moment. As soon as the cloud stopped, they buried themselves beneath a mound of stones which has been known ever since as Jentillarri (Stones of the Pagans).

One pagan did not bury himself. Many years passed by and that storytelling survivor became the announcer of Kixmi to all the Basque people.

Seven Days

Based on the tale 'The Birth of Kixmi and the Origin of Olentzero'. That particular story, of which this is a re-telling, was told to José Miguel de Barandiarán by a shepherd's helper, from Zaldibia, in Aralar in 1916

~

The light show dimmed and the musketry eased just in time for food.

The door opened and seven drenched Catalans walked in. They were the same ones as the night before when the dominoes had dominated. But now, they were shattered. Their eyes were saturated with light. There was fear there too. When your eyes are as full as theirs you have to just stand and stare, breathe for a while, and let the food, the drink, the silence and stillness act like peacemakers to the self. Caspar David Friedrich's *Wanderer above the Sea of Fog* (1818) had to do the same. I looked behind them. A sea of fog was rising from the ground like smoke from a cauldron. We closed the door and we were safe again.

After they had calmed down, my father and I started talking to them. We spent two hours comparing different words in different languages. Language eventually turned into a ritual of hand gestures, grins, and passing the breadbasket around again and again. Who needed French, Spanish and English? They looked a bit like knights. Not the knight-in-shining-armour type but the Celtic ones that Arthur originally had. Gwrhyr Gwalstawd Ieithoedd was one of my favourite Celtic knights. He was a shapeshifter and he could speak Welsh, Catalan, English and owl. Yes, he could speak with animals including the old Owl of Cwm Cawlwyd, the Ousel of Cilgwri, the Eagle of Gwern Abwy, the Stag of Redynfre, and my favourite, the Salmon of Llyn Llyw. In the old tales, he talks to these 'Oldest Animals' in their quest to find Mabon fab Modron who was taken from his mother at three nights old. One of the spectacled men looked like W.B. Yeats. I decided that he would be Gwrhyr. I christened the others Bedwyr, Cai, Menw, and so on. Dad was Arthur minus beard. My imagination started painting their faces in twirling blues and knots from *Gwalia Celtica*. They accepted my mental baptism as they drank their red wine.

Eog Llyn Llyw

These old knights had different names in the Pyrenees. They were the 'Wondrous Men'.[10] One of them flattened mountains by simply sitting down. In my head, John the Soldier was a very strong man like Bedwyr. One day, John met a man that stored no less than 1,250 pounds of wool in each nostril. They asked him why he kept so much wool up his nose, and he answered that it was a precaution to keep his breath inside. John asked for a demonstration. The man slowly unstopped one of his nostrils. No sooner was the nasal passage open that a great gust proceeded from it. All

10 See stories 'The Wondrous Men' and 'John the Soldier'. As told by Juan Mendizabal and Matias de Aranaz in the early 1920s.

the trees were knocked down and the hedges lost their leaves. What a force! I now understood why there weren't many trees up there. Other favourites are the knight that could hear a seed germinate and the sound of footsteps a hundred miles away, a knight that could run a hundred miles in a matter of minutes, and the fellow who drank up a whole river including a boat with people still in it. That last one developed such a bad bellyache after drinking that he eventually died.

Perhaps these Catalans were similar men. Dad was quiet that night. One of them tapped me on my shoulder. He spoke excellent English:

'Tell me, what are you doing here?' He smiled at me.

'Here, or?'

'No, the Pyrenees in general.'

'Dad's been coming here for years. He is introducing me, if you like.'

'This is good. Make most of it. My friends and I are heading to Aneto. We are much looking forward. We may see you somewhere afterwards. They say, you never meet only once in mountains. You understand?'

'I think so. I hope so.'

'Good. Then we will meet somewhere again.'

I smiled and started looking around. My eyes were getting heavier and the company and low-level conversation formed an apt soundtrack after a long day. The Catalan tapped my shoulder again.

'Did you know that man on your table yesterday?'

He sipped some wine.

'He's a man from Alsace and he's walking the GR10,' I answered.

'I know. We have seen him many times,' he lets out a giggle, 'he did not like the food, no?'

'He hated it!'

'Ha, it's the same tonight. Look, it's the apple pudding. It reminds me of baby food!'

'Yes… but I rather like it.' I watched his face turn into amazement.

'Really? You Welsh must be very poor!'

He translated what I'd said to his comrades and they all burst into laughter. The next thing, seven extra portions of apple appeared before my father and me. Dad started eating the apple pudding like he eats yogurt – very quickly. The guy continued as he stared at my father's unique way of eating,

'Have you met the Alsatian before?' he finished his wine.

'No. Why?'

'He's been travelling a long way. I think he is on some kind of *peregrinació*. You understand?' He was waving his hand around, drawing words.

'I think so. Pilgrimage?' I said. My father nodded.

'That's it… He told us one night about his daughter.' His face looked really serious.

'What about her?'

'It's a tragic story…'

~

The Tale of How Hemingway Lost his Daughter

Life is hard enough as it is and it becomes much harder when you lose a child. The seven of us were staying in another refuge when the man you call 'Hemingway' walked in. He seemed jolly enough, like at d'Espingo, but his eyes were sad. My friend asked him about his past and he told us about his job, his wife, all the usual stuff, before opening up about his daughter. Her name was Manon.

Manon studied literature at Toulouse. She was beautiful and intelligent and her father loved her more than all the other children. The time came for her to move away. She got a place in Toulouse and the only trouble was that she was now a long way from her father. Nevertheless, she moved away and she did extremely well in her studies.

One evening, Hemingway was snoring next to his wife. The phone rang. They ignored it. It rang a second time and he reluctantly woke up, sneezing twice, before slipping his hand out of the duvet. He grabbed the handset. His wife put the light on almost in accordance with all the stereotypes she had learnt from American movies. All she needed now was for him to tell her to 'go back to bed dear' or something like that.

'Who is this?' Hemingway asked.

'*Monsieur*?' a voice said.

'Yes?'

'This is the police… I am afraid we have some bad news for you… It's about your daughter.' He suddenly felt sick and he couldn't breathe for a few seconds.

'What is this about, officer?'

'I am very sorry. We have found a body in Spain and we believe it is your daughter. We need you to come and identify it.'

He finished the conversation before curling up on the mattress like the Hunchback of Notre Dame. He threw a glass of water at the wall. His wife entered a dark cave and rolled two great stones over the entrances. Her hands blocked the light and everything else out. Her husband went into the garden. It was dark, but he started watering the flowers with a trickling hosepipe. In the distance there were rabbits feeding on his lawn.

Manon's body had washed up on a beach in Spain. Hemingway never said where, because his eyes would always water up whenever he got to any of the details. He didn't know how this had happened and he definitely didn't know why. All he knew was that she was dead and the next couple of years would be purgatorial. His wife left him. Their grief was too much for each other. Manon meant so much to him. They'd named her after Marcel Pagnol's *Manon des Sources* which had been their favourite novel at university. He never imagined that it would be him that would be left alone with the goats and an old mouth organ.

The sea had taken her. The worst thing was that he dreamt that he was her. He dreamt that he could see himself sleeping and he would try and try to wake himself up and when he woke up all he could see was his own reflection in the black.

He is on a quest, and I doubt he will ever find what he is looking for.

~

The Catalan finished his story and filled his beaker up with red wine.

'He never found out what happened to her?' I was quite upset by the whole thing and needed to know more.

'Nothing. He said he didn't trust the Spanish police. He thinks she was stolen from him.'

In my head I imagined Hemingway reaching the sea, dropping his gear in the sand, and walking slowly into the waves.

The next thing I knew, one of the knights had brought out that little silk bag. He poured a wave of dominoes on the table, and for a minute, they looked like clattering runes. 'Aneto, here we come!' One of them cheered in public-school English. Dad left the table. He gets far too competitive.

That night I dreamt about my friend. I imagined him walking for miles out into the sea. All I could see was this head, bobbing like an island, never sinking, always moving. In my sleep I followed him in an old-fashioned boat surrounded by what looked like Celtic warriors with blue patterns on their skin. I asked them: 'Where are we going?' They looked at me as if I were stupid or dead. Hemingway's head grew huge and his eyes burnt yellow. I left the scene as sleep finally took over.

The evening and the morning were the second day.

The Border between France and Spain from 'Episcopatus Bala-bastrensis et comitatus Ribagorcae' (1850)

3

Flowers dense and keen as midnight stars aflame

'The Lake of Gaube' Algernon Charles Swinburne

Do you remember an Inn,
Miranda?
Do you remember an Inn?
And the tedding and the spreading
Of the straw for a bedding,
And the fleas that tease in the High Pyrenees,
And the wine that tasted of tar?

'Tarantella' Hilaire Belloc

As I continue through these Genesis valleys, I see the flowers burning like stars. I put my ear to the ground like Beethoven and listen to the melodies of the High Pyrenees. We are so often deaf to the sounds that matter. At first there is silence. But after a few seconds my ears adjust and I hear music of growth as seeds germinate. Others are fully grown and their petals act like Aeolian harps.

The Refuge de Portillon is situated next to a big lake. I was woken up by a different noise that morning and I noticed that the water had little waves on its surface. The sun was up and yet it wasn't quite daytime yet. I changed windows and saw a helicopter landing outside. Dad said something about how dangerous helicopters were. He was rolling his mat and it looked as if he were talking to that mat. The helicopter's doors flung open and men and women started jumping off, unclipping the supplies and giving the pilot thumbs up. I later learnt that these people were repairing the dam and not in the middle of the Korean War. I whistled the M*A*S*H theme tune as the helicopter took off like a big metal hornet.

The Catalans left early. We never really said goodbye but I watched them snake up the hill towards Spain. As they ascended, the sun got hotter and hotter. The light transformed the cliff face from a grey monochrome colour into a terracotta hue. Even the Catalan knights seemed to change. They were no longer Celtic warriors but *toreros* with their *traje des luces* (suit of lights). Their red and orange coats aided the metamorphosis and took me back to a bullfight that had stunned me as a child. I must have switched the television channel when my mother wasn't watching. There are three types of *toreros* or bullfighters. The *matador de toros* (killer of bulls), the *picador* who uses a lance called the *pica*, and the *banderillero* who plants the *banderilla*.

At first, I loved the costumes, the horses, the bull and the *toreros*. But I wasn't ready for what was coming. Slowly, the brutality unfolded as I watched them hurting the bull again and again and again. The sneaky *banderillero* with his weapons. Dart after dart. Red cloaks flapping, people clapping, animals wheeling, before the silence of an intermission enveloped the bloody stage. He stops. He starts again. Running, bleeding, breathless, furious to the last, until finally, Byron's 'lord of lowing herds' sinks like a ship in the sand. A sword was sheathed in his body like a returned Excalibur just where the neck mingled with the spine. Of the three types of bullfighter, I can remember hating the *banderillero* much more than the *picador* or *matador* because he plants the *banderilla*. Something horrible had happened and I wept for that bull. I felt the same way in my first year in secondary school as we gathered in the concrete grove behind the canteen. My friends stood there, some silent, some cheering whilst others just passed by. A *banderillero* of a boy came into the centre of a ring with his hands closed around something. His glittering eyes lowered and we followed his gaze until we saw a toad sitting on his palm. I remember a young *matador* being forced into the centre by vulgar eyes; his eyes were damp. He took the toad from the *banderillero* and hurled the poor creature into the sky. It landed with a thud. The *matador* hated himself; he was like *Chicuelo* who never wanted to kill the bulls.[11] But that *banderillero* enjoyed it. His eyes, his stance, and his whole being repulsed me whilst the experience made me a sadder and wiser man. I looked up at the hill and changed the *toreros* back into Celtic knights again.

Beyond the warm colours of the cliff, the snow looked white hot. I felt edgy but my hunger took that edge away. Breakfast is usually medieval bread, sweet plum jam, cardboard crackers (or a madeleine), and a big bowl of coffee. If you're lucky you might get some honey. Dad was pasting honey onto a cracker like a plasterer happy with his work. His lips enjoyed every mouthful and the map got stickier and stickier. But he didn't care and neither did I. We were both like bears, Baloo-like, enjoying Mother Nature's recipes. Meanwhile the Germans were ready to go. We quickly ate our food and eventually left with the two Germans towards the Vallon de Literole Inferior.

Bits of the path were steep and you had to hold on to a cable as you walked along the edges. After about an hour of cairn following we approached the alabaster slope which headed up towards the col. The sun illuminated its edge like a razor blade and the chiaroscuro created by the rock and snow would have made an excellent photograph. The surface was hard and I could hear running water underneath the white. The Germans passed us and continued up the hill.

11 *Chicuelo* - A matador from Seville who hated killing bulls. His real name was Manuel Jiménez Moreno (1902-1967).

'River?' I looked at Dad,

'Yes. Make sure you stay clear of the dirty snow. You'll be able to tell if it's thinner.'

Navigating the edge of glaciers or ice is all about colour. One must be attentive to the different shades of white that reveal the thickness of your path.

'Come on Nay-fan. (Dad's cockney strengthened according to how recently he'd spoken to somebody from the South-East) We haven't got all day. It'll be good to get as much of this done as possible now.'

'Dad, I'm a bit giddy. It's the ice and this river under me.'

'Oh come, you big girl. It's a stream.'

'It's all right for you. You've got proper boots.'

'You don't need 'em.'

'Well that's logical. Look around!'

'Nigh-fun, they cost a shed load of money and you've got good ones on,' he looked at my feet, 'you're fine when you ski, what's the difference?'

'Psychological.'

'Nonsense.'

Nathan, (not 'Nigh-fun' or 'Nay-fun') was a prophet in the Bible. I saw what was coming too.

'This is good going… your boots are alright… not long now.'

'Dad.'

'What?'

'I'm in the hill.'

He turned round and saw his slightly overweight son being swallowed by the mountainside. One minute I was walking at a leisurely pace. The next moment, my whole leg went straight through the snow and I suddenly felt the running water filling my boot.

'The water's in my boots… do something!'

'Oh, Ney-fan, you're holding me back.'

'Give me your stick then…'

My father pulled me out with great inconvenience to himself but I think he enjoyed the pause. I sat on a rock, squeezing my wet sock, prophesying about blisters, boots, sore hips and long days. Dad stood on another rock laughing.

By now, the Germans were gone. The last I saw of them was one of them tying a bandana around the other one's head. I think one of them was definitely what is commonly known as a ski or a mountain 'bum.' These are an unusual people. You can recognise them by their birdcall, using words like 'cool', 'wicked', and 'awesome.' The Ski Bum usually spends a long time working for low wages and getting months of skiing in exchange. In the summer, they metamorphose into mountain-bums and they share selfies of each other camping on ridges with their go-pro cameras. They drink a lot, their hair is usually unusual, and they sometimes even walk, ski, or hike to a soundtrack which comes from their backpacks. They also talk an awful lot. If you meet one, be sure to have an excuse ready. Otherwise, they will detain you with an hour and a half of stories, show you ten thousand Facebook pictures, use the word 'sick' too many times, and start clicking their fingers in the air as if trying to eradicate some sticky toffee from their hands. I don't think we are mountain- or ski-bums. I only use the word 'sick' when I am ill.

The leg-in-the-mountain incident had caused us to fall behind. I was moody and I started remembering again. As a younger child I hated walking. The thought of going uphill was always coupled with dampness and pain and I can't remember when that moaning turned into enjoyment. What I do remember is coming home after a long, wet, walk: fogged-up glasses, steam coming up from my shoes, smell of mam's casserole, and Wyn, the ginger cat welcoming us home. It was a medley of chocolate-box covers. In the winter, our hallway was coloured by the stained glass window at the centre of the house. This light was my mother's work. Within it, people walked barefoot on an ancient pathway. Some of them were old and some were young while in their midst a figure sat on a horse. I used to stare at their faces and empathise with them. 'I know how you feel,' I used to tell them. I didn't think that it was fair that one of them had a horse, especially when the older people had to walk. People would come over to our house and say: 'Is that man Jesus?' They had a look of disgust, or usually, a polite Protestant frown. Mam would answer, 'No, it's a copy of a smaller window at Canterbury Cathedral depicting pilgrims on the road to Canterbury.' She was well rehearsed. Some folk called her a heretic for making a graven image. She was telling the truth, though. As I grew up the window changed. I placed swaying palm leaves into the hands of the medieval pilgrims. I changed the mounted pilgrim into that curious figure who rode into Jerusalem on a braying ass. I changed that nameless pilgrim into the depiction that I'd seen in my picture Bible. That window meant so much to me.

Our kitchen was always full of light. Our kitchen was like the old *aelwyd* which is much more than just a hearth. In ancient times the fire never went out. The task of *enhuddo* (covering) and *dadenhuddo* (uncovering) has always been very important in Celtic countries. The seed of yesterday's fire, the ember, is kept as the core for the next day's fire. Our kitchen retained something of these older traditions even though the fire has long gone. In my mind, my mother is always sitting there; her back bent like a monk illuminating Jesus pictures on the glass. My grandparents are there too on the pair of parker knolls in the corner. The cat is high on the dresser dreaming of jungles and the land of mice which is above him in the attic. As a treat, (small rodent lovers please skip this bit) Dad would let Wyn have an hour living his dream in the attic. We'd hear a lot of noise and Wyn would return a happy cat.

The col was getting closer. We slowly aimed for the point where the Germans had crossed and when we finally got there, it seemed a bit mundane. Reaching a col can be an anti-climax. You spend an hour or more snaking your way towards that line and when you reach it, it is usually disappointing. There is either another col further ahead or the view is not what it should be after such an effort. But sometimes it is phenomenal. The col is another God-drawn border. The weather changes there; you can feel the temperature rising or falling as you pass a certain point. The best thing is climbing in hot, sultry air and then reaching a col where the cool wind blasts the heat away. These moments are best felt when sitting down where you can watch the mountains move. This happens slowly but if you wait long enough you can feel the ground shifting beneath you, inch by inch.

Col near Pic La Néouvielle

If the weather is good, col-sitting is brilliant. I am not interested in peak-bagging like my father but I am interested in the mountains. What will become of a world that does not know its mountains? I wait for the unexpected. I hope that there will be something extra around each corner and if there is not, I am content with the slow shift of the hills, the smell of dry terrain, and the artistic structure of the flora and fauna. The sun lights it all up and turns me into a Pyrenean with my brown skin and fair hair. At night time I fall in love with the moon whether she is a swallow – thin and bright like the crest of a col – or that sombre boat sailing in a black sea. One side is bright and fair whilst the faint shimmering of the other half is like the movements of a hidden body revealed in splendour when the wheel is full.

From the col, you see that trees are rare in high places. But there are valleys in the Pyrenees which are lush and full of herbs: such places smell wonderful. I remember walking towards Vignemale and passing through a long valley filled with flowers. You half expected the flowers to gather up and form figures in the green or create a menagerie of magical creatures. God made men out of dust but the Celts believed that young women could be fashioned from petals and leaves. Gwydion whispered to the flowers of oak, the flowers of the broom and the flowers of the meadowsweet and commanded them to gather and form the fairest maiden Wales had ever seen. They named her Blodeuwedd because her face blossomed like a flower. I started thinking whether the Pyrenees had a Gwydion. If so, these creations would be smaller because of the flowers, each petal a pixel. What would Gwydion use if he came there? June orchids? There are twenty-two varieties in the Pyrenees. There are Alpine snowbells (*Soldanela alpina*), large flowered and long-leaved butterworts (*Pinguicula longifolia*), and the Oreja de Oso (*ramonda myconi*) too. The oreja looks like an African violet but smaller with flowers that jewel the rock and grass. Everything small is special, because they are set against the big scale of the mountains. My favourite flower is the Purple Saxifrage (*Saxifraga oppositifolia*) which grows in the rock. The Latin 'Saxifrage', despite its size, means 'Stone-breaker.' I first tasted this nutty flower in a salad prepared for me in Refuge La Soula in the Valleé de Louron. André Font-Lapalisse, the guardian there, said that all the food had come from the valley; he had collected the Saxifrage himself. Even the lamb had been sold to him by the local shepherd. We sat with the guardian and with a scientist who was spending a month analysing butterflies. The French call butterflies *papillon* which is one step away from the Welsh *pili-pala*; both are better names than butterfly. The scientist's English was poor but he showed us his samples, and his net which was a cross between the Child Catcher's in *Chitty Chitty*

Bang Bang and my father's shrimp net in the garage. We had a good meal. Hemingway would have liked the food there because it was a good house.

Refuge La Soula where I first tasted Saxifrage

Dad investigated something green on the col. The wind began to howl. He half thought about pocketing it, but after a moment, decided not to. Instead, he lay down and closed his eyes in tiredness. Even taking a cutting was too much effort. The signs always forbid flower picking. But now and again, Dad sneakily takes cuttings from his favourites which he hopes to nurture back home. This usually ends up in disaster. He took some Saxifrage once and tried planting it in our garden. The flowers soon disappeared and I imagined some blackbird or cuckoo enjoying the aniseed taste. The same thing happened when he retrieved a tiny cactus from the Grand Canyon. He carefully wrapped it in a sock before sneaking it through customs (thank goodness they didn't find it). He lovingly planted the little ball in a plant pot high up in his study where other Wyevale cacti lived. The next day, Wyn the cat passed the breakfast table with the cactus in his mouth. My father was horrified but my sister and I thought it was hilarious.

We were getting colder and colder on the col. The only living thing was the moss that dragged itself reluctantly across the rock. I was reluctant as well. My feet were in a bad way and I knew I would probably fail to climb the next peak, the Pic de Perdiguero at 3200m. I looked at my watch and it seemed to melt on my arm like a Dali. There were no animals. I waited for them so I could re-name them like in the beginning.

A gush of wind sent us on our way but that memory would be clocked, as all are, somewhere in our own Bodleian.

After bum-skidding down a steep bit, we could see the junction where a decision would have to be made. The path skirted alongside a turquoise lake that mirrored the mountains in its orb. As I walked around, I admired how blue it all was and how the colour of the lake changed, depending on the sky's hue. The rocks around the lake were marble white and we were both in red coats. I like thinking about half-aquatic worlds. As the white stone entered the lake, it suddenly became distant and different although it was still stone. There was a singularity to the whole scene as the mountain was reflected in the water. At home, Capel Celyn, Atlantis and *Cantre'r Gwaelod* are now glassy expanses. Once upon a time, these had been the routes taken to the otherworld or marshlands where flat bottomed boats moved silently across sounds and estuaries. The Vikings sent their dead on burning barges whilst the Celts threw swords and corpses into the deep. Sometimes a hand would take up the offered sword and re-present it to the world as a changed and magical implement. In the Pyrenees, water is very cold because it is usually formed by melting snow. There is something frightening in a lake that is completely empty. Some of these places are even too cold for fish.

My mother's family are from north Wales and my grandparents lived there when Liverpool drowned one of our villages. I remember my grandfather telling me about the church, the gravestones and the houses entombed at the bottom of the lake. Although they bulldozed everything, I imagined that there was an otherworld carrying on underwater. As a child, I thought that the people were still there. I conjured turquoise church services in my mind with the burials in blue. Fish swimming between the pews and a coral reef forming around the organ. In my dreams I'd post letters through rusty letter boxes. I'd open doors that stirred up sandy clouds from the bed whilst any noise echoed on like a lonely low 'c' on a cello. Such dark spaces haunted my dreams. Places undisturbed by the old lamps, family bibles, ghostly photographs and clothing eerily floating like seaweed. Perhaps one day, the whole of Wales will sink under the sea. An archipelago will form from the highest peaks: Idris, Wyddfa, the Arans and the Brecon lowlands. Anything green would be worth keeping and we would guard our trees like Gondor. We would write stories and songs about woodlands and gardens, fruit trees and cacti that grew in drier places.

We would dive
down
deep into the water

deeper
deeper
and deeper still.
Out of the blue,
the weathercock
the tiles
the chimneys
the hollowed eyes of windows
deeper
crumbling brickwork
deeper
the weathered stones of the chapel steps
deeper
the empty roads, no vehicles, no lights, nothing; miles and miles of sunken roads going here, there, and everywhere – but nowhere.

The divers would find something light or memorable to bring up. But like in a toy shop, there is too much to choose from and they'd emerge with tales of lonely farmhouses and road signs pointing to places where nobody goes anymore. It was like a series of dreams, one after the other, image after image. But nothing came to the top. Everything stayed down and came to a permanent stop.

This was a strange lake. Maybe this was the spot where Odin lobbed his eye into the deep.

We continued around the lake and followed the

cairns up to a little stone grove which sheltered us from the wind.

'How are you feeling?

'Not good.'

'Take the goose down and sit over here'.

Dad gave me his goose-down jacket and I sat on the rock. I was depressed. I was young and yet my body had failed. Like Gawain, my strength seemed to wax and wane with the mounting and sinking of the sun. Dad put his hood up and carried on. I half expected him to turn into a bird, like Gwalchmai, and fly towards the peak where his wings would slow down before wrapping themselves around his own body again, keeping himself warm like Placidus the monk.

I slept for an hour and a half. In my dreams, all I seemed to be doing was climbing or falling. Like Jeremiah in my children's Bible, I'd lift my head and see sheer cliffs, crags, deep holes or sinkholes, all merging into darkness. I'd fall a long way and pass mountaineering prophets burdened with ice axes and ropes, prancing chamois, desolate villages, vineyards – whole worlds. The peak would get smaller and smaller as I fell. The swish of a vulture's wing, or the moist droplets in every cloud, added a tint of reality to the scenes like shadows in a painted masterpiece. But the sun, like an orange eye – still and eternal – was strangely distant and unreal. Everything around it swirled in evanescence but the solar being remained still. I'd hit the ground and wake up sweating. I'd feel around me. The cold rock of Jeremiah's well would change into my stony pillow. I touched the moss which confirmed that I was awake. I was sitting at 2900m and the cold had shaken me up. Food is important at this point. I looked in my bag. Babybel cheeses in red wax, two cans of tuna fish in brine, *saucisson,* boiled sweets and a pack of biscuits. I gobbled a cheese and some fish before tending to my feet. The boots came off after a struggle and I walked down to a bit of greenery which had become boggy from the lake. It was like walking on a giant sponge and it was lovely. My feet were soothed and cleansed at the same time.

Dad returned after a couple of hours. He was happy because this was the second time that he'd climbed that peak (he likes to try these mountains in different conditions). I know he is a Munro bagger but sometimes I do worry about him. There was one time when I caught him in his study looking at two photographs of different summit tops:

'What are you doing, Dad?'

'I'm checking whether I reached the real summit.'

'Why?'

'Because that peak has two tops which are only twenty yards away from one another.'

I felt puzzled. In my head that would count but he

could not tick his little book unless he had actually touched the top of the cairn. Why do we do that when we get to the top of a hill? The more I think about cairns, the more I question their use. Our eyes look for them when we should be looking around. We are determined to touch them even though so many are the simple time-wasting doodles of bored mountaineers on the hillside. Over the years, climbers reach out for the cairn in thanksgiving. They rest a while and lean their backs on its structure before going down. Others come and place a stone on the cairn. These people leave their colonising mark on the hillside. Even though some cairns are knocked down over time, their column-like presence holds up the sky. When people move on or simply pass away into new territories, the cairns will still be marking the hillsides like antiquarian columns.

'Minas Morgul' Col

We left the spongy arbour and walked down to another col which looked like Minas Morgul. The two hills bordering the col were jagged and black. No moss. No heather. No life. Dad stood between the two hills like a spectre. I took a photograph on my phone. It succeeded in portraying a tired landscape interrupted by life. The sentinel hills dominate whilst my father is barely recognisable. The next part of the walk would be one of the worst descents in the seven days. We looked over the edge, and streets of large boulders lay before us. It was so steep, and each gap looked deep and dangerous. We spent an hour jumping rock to rock, hitting my blister each time while my ankles felt ready to snap. When we reached the end of the boulders, a steep grassy bit flowed out from underneath the rocks. I was encouraged at first. Grass is usually where you rest; he makes me lie down in green pasture Psalm 23 kind of thing. Little things like this matter a great deal in the mountains. My feet welcomed the change of terrain but as soon as I stepped on the grass I slipped back onto my two hands. In the Pyrenees, the high grass is very sharp and dangerous because you can't get hold of it when you fall. When you do grab it, it's like being stabbed with mini lances, leaving your palms with bloody spots which begin to itch. I relied on my backside, slipping through the brooks, avoiding the sharp grass and embracing the rock face with my whole being. My body was a piece of art by the end, streaked and painted with the red, greens and browns. I looked back and cursed the 'Minas Morgul' col, its boulder field and the spiteful grass.

~

Mount Gilboa

Under the tamarisk tree at Jabesh they bury the bones of a royal family. The king's name was Saul and he had a son called Jonathan. David Son of Jesse looks up and curses the mountain where it occurred:

91

'I curse you Gilboa. I curse the ground and the very clouds that adorn your peak. I curse the trees, the shrubs, and the cairns. May you be a desolate place forever! You are stained by the blood of Jonathan, my closest friend and brother!'

The warriors weep as they feel the dry soil slip through their fingers onto the blackened bones of their sovereign.

King Saul had been a foolish king and had ignored the commands of YAHWEH. The night before he died, he climbed up to a cave in *En Dor* and consulted a wise woman who lived there. She was old, so old, that it frightened Saul. At first, she didn't recognise the hooded king. Saul's climbing companions addressed her:

'The king wishes a demonstration.'

'My lords, the king has forbidden my art.'

With these words, the king pulled his hood down, and said 'The king will allow you this time. I swear that no harm will come to you.'

She recognised him and thought about all the possible escape routes. His eyes commanded her to begin.

'If this is no trick, I will do what you ask. Who do you want to call from the otherworld?'

'Samuel, Prophet of YAHWEH.' He hid in the rock expecting his old mentor to appear in a flash. But it took some time. The witch was uncomfortable because she had feared the prophet when he was alive. The darkness slowly enveloped her as she started talking in the old tongue. Her wrinkles filled in and her eyes glittered again. Her flesh became soft. Her hair blackened like ink spreading in white water. She uttered the unutterable:

and waited for something to rise up.

That's when Saul saw something. She cut herself and

the

drops

of

blood

drew

up

up

up

the spirit up, drop by drop, inch by inch. She fell in a heap and started talking on the spirit's behalf. Samuel's last prophesy did not comfort the King.

The next day, the battle turned against Saul. His eyes didn't blink. He waited for the arrow, the sharp cold steel, the spear, the axe or the stone from the sling. It didn't come.

'Fight father!' The voice of his son, Jonathan, 'Father, the men need you!'

'I am undone boy!'

'Father, inspire them!' Jonathan pleaded.

'I'm undone,' he whispered to himself as he surveyed the carnage.

'Father!' Jonathan fought like a wondrous man. He serenaded with death and clung to life with the edge of his sword. He painted the field red before death stopped the dance. He turned one last time: 'Father! Fight!' And as he shouted, the beloved of Israel was stabbed in the back. He died.

Saul's mouth opened with unutterable grief. His hair whitened as the seconds ticked by and the Philistines stained Gilboa with the blood of the chosen. The king rode away and the men of Israel fled.

'My lord... archers!' His armour bearer shouted. The royal guards fell like leaves from a wind-swept tree. Only the armour bearer remained. 'My lord, take your sword!'

For a moment, Saul remembered the days of his youth. He stands tall again. His grip tightens around the hilt. His tears mix with sweat. He kills one, two, three... But the archers fire their shafts

One  hit.
Two hit.
Three hit.

Saul calls his servant:

'Draw your sword, and thrust me through with it, lest these uncircumcised men come and thrust me through and abuse me.'

The Philistines gather round and watch.

'I cannot, my lord. I will not', his voice breaks as the king snaps one of the shafts that pierced him. The armour bearer took the crown. Saul fell on his sword. The armour bearer dropped the crown and followed the king across the threshold.

This is why David cursed Mount Gilboa under the tamarisk tree at Jabesh.

Based on the accounts found in 1 Samuel 28-31
and 1 Chronicles 10

~

Hours passed and my father walked further and further ahead. We passed some stony cabins. Shepherd-built bridges eased our way, and the odd tree started to surprise us at random points on the path. It was like being at the beginning again as small trees turned into middle-size ones. Then they became a bit more varied as we crossed into Spain. (I don't know where the border is but decided that the boulders must have been near the imaginary line.) We walked lower and lower and the trees grew bigger and stronger. Before long they were up to my shoulders and some flowers appeared in their shade. Now and again a mushroom looked temptingly at us saying 'eat me' but then its purple underbelly showed.

Eventually, the trees introduced us to a river. I offered my hands to the water and soaked them in the Estos. The Rio was as sonorous as the birds that bordered its banks. I felt like an intruder in Eden. Horses grazed on the hillside, their tails brushing the flies away with elegance. There was a warmer yellowish colour to the grass and you could see the green veins in the ground spreading life around the river. Our presence was like an unwelcome breath on a pane of clear glass, disturbing everything and trampling on sacred ground. My father stepped on the branches and I left footprints on the dampened path which nobody had trodden on for a while. I imagined descending doves, lepers washing seven times, parting waters, floating axes, and purple-clad women praying on the banks. And then there were some trees which might be myrtles. Their branches formed a frame, and in the middle, a man was standing there like a gardener.

I blinked and only branches, gaps, and a memory remained. Dad was cursing a root that he'd just tripped over. The plants looked foreign as we walked further away from France. We had not seen a living person since Portillon except for the horses, marmots and the odd vulture which followed us like flies. And when we entered the forest, the flies started bothering us more than vultures ever could. Horse flies bit and ticks tried their best to attach themselves to my leg. Other flies landed on our noses and were determined to get into our mouths or nostrils. Even the soft grass turned into nettles as Beethoven's Pastoral slowly changed into something discordant and ugly. This was becoming a long day. We had been walking since 7 a.m. and it was now about 5:45 in the afternoon. My body fought and longed for water, recovery, and rest. Walking through the woodland was becoming more difficult because I was tripping over the roots that had inconveniently occupied the paths. This way had not been used for a long time. The cairns had completely disappeared and there were no painted signs; we were simply following the river which twisted and turned like a snake. Then it started raining.

We reached a little signpost indicating that we were close to Refugio de Estós. Ahead of us, there was a strange-looking path, steep but eerily paved. There is always something mystical about the sudden interruption of man on a landscape, especially in the form of a good path. But the rainfall was making it slippery. I could feel the pain beginning to show on my face and my imagination started painting again. Hot baths, Egyptian cotton sheets. Back to those floral valleys of earlier today. Before madness took over, I saw our third refuge appear. Its square building was surrounded by mooing cows.

'I'll go ahead to see if we can book dinner,' Dad called to me from ahead.

'Ok, get me a Fanta, will you'.

The Refugio de Estós is 1895m high and run by twin brothers. One of them is a dairy farmer who uses the basement to keep his quad bikes. He was the first human that I encountered in Spain and he bore more than a passing resemblance to Bill Sikes. He passed me and grunted 'Hola!' A pair of dogs followed him; one of them looked like Sikes' Bull's Eye and the other one looked ill. Bull's Eye had one eye and he took a disliking to me from the outset. They both sniffed me before jumping away when Bill Sikes called them. My father re-emerged from the building with a can of Fanta Naranja which sounded wonderful. My favourite word in Italian is *Prego*, and *Naranja* had definitely got the award for Spanish.

From the outside, this refuge was a little different from the others. To begin with, it seemed deserted. The only sound I could hear was the distant bark of Bull's Eye and the clattering beads that covered the doorway. I sat on a bright blue bench and waited for my father. When your eyes are tired, the mountains seem to fold in on themselves. I guess it's a kind of mirage. I thought about Hemingway and the Catalans. I imagined them all playing dominoes in a shepherd's hut. I tried to imagine their faces but found that I couldn't do it, apart from some features such as spectacles, a big nose, and the sound of their voices. Hemingway, though, was different. I could see him clearly. His voice still rang in my ear and his moustache was still moving up and down because his conversation went on even after he'd left the place. Why did he remain in my memory while the Catalans were drifting away? My father re-emerged from behind the beads and beckoned me inside.

The place smelled of incense. I hate incense. 'This is a bit grim, Pa.'

'It's okay… but I'm warning you… the food isn't great.'

We passed a row of school-like lockers which made a clatter as we walked by. They tolled for the luckless walkers who had to suffer the food in the place.

'How do you know?'

'Because I remember from the last time I was here.'

'I didn't know you'd been here.' We entered the kitchen/dining area. I didn't feel well at all. It was very dark inside. It looked a bit like a Tibetan sanctuary minus the friendly orange monks. Prayer flags adorned the walls and the place was dusty and old-fashioned. Inside the dining hall was a little hole in the wall surrounded by postcards and photographs.

'There's another one, by the way', Dad said in a whisper.

'What do you mean?'

'I mean the twin.'

One twin lived indoors and the other was always outside. We were standing by a little hole in the wall. We rang an annoying little bell and the indoor-twin's face popped out from his home. He was a discontented man determined to do as little work as possible. Unfair? You'd understand if you'd have been there. He looked at us as if we were dirty. For all I knew, he did not have legs. All I saw was his grumpy face accompanied by his grumpy shoulders which acted like his mouth. You said something like:

'We've had a long day,' then a silence. He understood English but only answered with a shrug of the shoulder.

'Do you think the rain will continue?' Shrug of the shoulder.

'Do you have a bin?' Shrug.

'Thank you.' Shrug.

He wore a medieval-style hat and an apron which looked like he'd bought it second-hand from a slaughterhouse. As soon as we sat down, he put the telly on and turned it right up. He wasn't deaf because his brother shouted at him from outside and he answered it in a quick, loud sentence accompanied by an annoying hesitation which transformed him into an 'Eeeehhhh what's up Doc?' Bugs Bunny kind of guy. I looked at Dad and even he shrugged his shoulders.

Two blonde youngsters were eating a Pot Noodle on one of the tables. My father had already met the pair and he informed me that they were Czech. I sat down and they offered me some strong stuff which I refused. They then gave me some medicine which helped a lot; I think it was herbal. She was definitely the Norse goddess Freyja and he was her brother Freyr. I sat in that chair for ages watching Freyja and Freyr gobble their noodles. I felt sick, tired and dizzy and I longed for the evening to end. I can remember a middle-aged French couple coming in and sitting as far away from us as they possibly could. I must have looked really unpleasant, a cross between a bad piece of modern art and someone struck by the plague. The little bell rang, indicating that our meal was ready. Hemingway thought d'Espingo was bad. He had obviously never been to Estós.

We were handed a silver platter along with some bread, wine and water. On the platter, there was some sort of rice pudding right next to meatballs, a green stodgy vegetable (which nearly finished me off) and some boiled potatoes which looked like purple boils. I've had some bad meals in the past but this was grim. It tasted awful and I must have washed it down with enough Naranja to make me orange. I wasted half of it and did a Stan Laurel by hiding the remains of the *repas* into my cup topped with a napkin (I'd learnt this from my grandfather).

'You can't do that,' Dad was speaking through the gaps in his teeth.

'I'm ill.'

'No I mean stuffing it all in a cup. He's going to find out anyway.'

The guardian looked at me as if there was a bad

smell in the room. I said '*Je suis malade*.' He nodded, shrugged, and snatched the tray off me. I wish I had the guts to pick those meatballs up and start lobbing them around the room in disgust. I needed Hemingway!

The Czechs were happy, anyway. For about an hour, I listened to them whistle and sing as they washed their dishes. I imagined that I was sitting in Uncle's wooden cabin from *War and Peace*. I could almost hear the sound of the guitar and feel the heat that can only be felt when it is numbingly cold outside. The Czech girl's singing reminded me of Natasha. I half expected her to run out and dance with those unteachable and inimitable Russian movements that Uncle had expected of the young Countess. But the sight of Magwitch, or rather Bill Sikes, soon dashed that dream. I was back. I felt sick and night had swallowed the sun. Dad came in:

'It's a bit grim.'

'What?'

'The bedroom. It's one of the highest bunk beds I've seen. Fortunately, there aren't too many people staying here. How are you feeling?'

'Bad. Those brothers creep me out.'

'Try and be kind.'

'Mhhm.'

The bedroom was dark and the bunk bed was, as reported, four storeys high. We went up on the second bunk and I slowly drifted into sleep, conscious of Dad next to me fiddling with the batteries in his head torch. I slept like a sloth, not knowing who was above us on the third or fourth storey. I must have been really ill that night because my dreams were vivid and very strange.

~

The Tale of Hemingway and Makilakixki

Aita bat iru semekin bizi ementzan. They say a father lived here with his three sons. Hemingway was one of those young men. The house was a wooden one and his father was an ageing one. He was coming of age and being offered work by a local squire. He served on the man's estate for a couple of years. Time flew and his master was very impressed by his hard work and strength which he applied in the house and on the grounds. In my dream, I saw the master bringing a *burro* and handing it to Hemingway:

'This is for you, amigo. Look after the *burro* and he will look after you'.

'What do you mean?'

'This is a unique *burro*. All you say is "give me gold" and the *burro* will immediately produce it. He has made me very rich and I wish to share my good fortune with others.'

Hemingway was thrilled and I saw him picking up

some *oro* where there should have been dung. He left the rich master and made his way home along a steep paved road.

As he travelled, he came across an inn called Refugio de Estós. As I slept, I looked through the window of the refuge and saw my father sitting down. I was there too, drinking some *Naranja* with Freyja and Freyr; our eyes were all aglow. Next to Freyja was her battle swine, Hildisvíni. Freyr had grown a huge blonde beard dotted with star-like jewels here and there. Both had bronze skin and life pulsated from heads to toes. In the other corner, the twin brothers greeted Hemingway whilst their dog growled at the *burro*.

Before bed, Hemingway became drunk. He walked over to the window in the wall and rang the bell before vomiting everywhere. It was all very loud and I covered my ears in my sleep. The window opened and Hemingway started warning the innkeeper:

'Don't even think of ssssaying "Give me gold" to my *burro*!' He giggled and burped at the same time. As soon as Hemingway was snoring on the bench, the innkeeper approached the donkey and took advantage of its secret: 'Give me gold' he whispered as the inn slept. At that moment the *burro* produced an abundance of gold on the dark floor. The shrewd innkeeper called his brother from the field.

'Replace this with one of ours,' he whispered as the other brother's eye sparkled whilst staring at the gold.

The *burro* was replaced and the innkeeper stored the gold in his kitchen cupboard.

The following morning, Hemingway did not notice any change except for a throbbing headache. He paid the innkeeper and embraced my father, offering me a cigarette, which he said would help my writing. He left and proceeded towards his father's house.

As soon as he reached his home he called his father and his brothers together.

'You will not believe my good fortune! The gods have blessed me with such a gift!'

He called for a sheet and prepared to conjure up the golden waste. The donkey looked lost and he broke wind because he was so nervous.

'Give me gold!' He shouted like Harpagon from Molière's *L'Avare (The Miser)*. The *burro* did not produce any gold. He said it again and again and even threw in an abracadabra but nothing happened – not even a rabbit. Well, something did happen. The *burro* broke wind and the sheet was covered in dung.

Later, the second son went away to work as a servant. The strange thing is that he looked just like Hemingway, only without the moustache. This one had an Abraham Lincoln beard. Similarly, he was a hard worker and his master awarded him with a magical table that had mysterious qualities. If he said 'Prepare dinner', it obeyed, and in doing so offered complete table service as well as food. This was fantastic and the food tasted even better than the best meal you've ever eaten. Hemingway's brother returned to his father's house, stopping in the inn half way. This time, the group of Catalans were staying there too and they treated Hemingway's brother to wine and dominoes. He, too, became a little merry and before bed he warned the innkeeper:

'Don't even think of saying to my table "Prepare dinner."'

Night fell and the lords slept deeply. (Imagine that scene in C.S. Lewis's T*he Voyage of the Dawn Treader* on the Island of Ramandu where Mavramorn, Revilian and Argoz (three of the Seven Noble Lords of Narnia) have been asleep for seven years.) They looked as if they would never wake and it would take a prince from a distant land to stir them from their sleep. The innkeeper couldn't believe his luck. He was being given all these goodies for nothing and he was actually getting away with it. He tiptoed to the table and pronounced the magic words 'prepare me dinner' and as he did so the table gleamed with flickering candlelight, its smell hit his nostrils, and he saw the meats, fruit and sauces. The innkeeper grinned in the night and called for his brother again:

'Herrrrmano!' He shouted quietly. 'Hermano!' With a bit more force. His brother came back with his two dogs panting,

'Replace the table, quick!'

The second brother left the sleeping lords and continued his journey home. He had bought a pair of mules to transport the table back. The caravan arrived. The father must have been frustrated when the brother approached the door with a so-called magical table. Had his sons completely lost their minds? Brother number two even managed to damage his father's house as he moved the table in. The mules met the donkey and they greeted one another with some braying. Meanwhile the brother was banging the table like a madman:

'Prepare me dinner! Make me dinner! Dinner, please, you stupid piece of wood!' The father shook his head. 'If your mother could see you now; peace be upon her.'

He stopped the banging and the shouting. It was an awkward meal that night.

Finally, the youngest brother went to work as a servant. Once again, he was the spitting image of Hemingway but he was about three feet shorter. (I think I must have laughed in my sleep at the thought.) When he finished his year of work, his master gave him a stick which looked old and heavy. This object also had extraordinary powers. He had only to pronounce the word 'Makilakixki' in the presence of the stick, and it would begin fighting everybody in the vicinity except for its young owner.

Funnily enough, the youngest son also stayed a

night at Estós. That night he was alone. He ate his meal quietly and he inquired from the innkeeper about the fine food that he was receiving.

'This stuff is good.'

'Many thanks. The food has all been sourced in the valley. I bought the lamb from a shepherd.' He was lying of course.

'Excellent. This has been a good day and this is a good house!'

'Yes?' The innkeeper suspected what was coming.

'Indeed. This meal is a fitting end. I have been given this staff by my master' (the third brother was kind-hearted and quite innocent) 'and it has extraordinary power!'

The innkeeper's ears stood up like the *burro* braying in the yard.

'What do you mean?'

'I don't quite understand it all,' the brother was honest, 'but apparently... well... my friend... Just don't address my stick by the name "Makilakixki" or you will regret it.' He was telling the truth.

'Don't worry, I won't!' The innkeeper lied again. His head filled with power, riches and the end of his miserable time as an innkeeper. As soon as the youngest brother went for a walk, he tiptoed up to the stick and shouted: 'Makilakixki!' Before the last syllable had rolled off his tongue, the stick stood upright on the paving stone. It shook. It banged the floor like it had been possessed by a demon. The innkeeper became worried and started crying out for his twin. 'Herrrmano!' The rod started whacking the Spaniard until he was bleeding and bruised. His bones were being cracked and he started shouting for the third brother. They both came through the door and saw the punishing rod bashing his host. The innkeeper begged him to stop it. He did.

After these events, the innkeeper confessed his sins. The rod had punished him and it showed him how vile he had been throughout his life. The young man demanded that the innkeeper return the *burro* and the stolen table or else the stick would continue to punish the innkeeper. The rascal returned what he had stolen and he was grieved at what he had done. The story ends with forgiveness.

Based on the Basque folktale, Makilakixki. The original story was told by Felipe Apalategui, from Atáun, in 1921

~

I woke up thinking about my strange dream and I started wondering where Hemingway was at that point. I imagined him carrying a great load upon his back, his clothes stained with time and his face blackened by so much cigarette smoke. The Catalans told us that he would sometimes stay on his own in the shepherd huts. Hemingway was probably still sleeping, making the most of being left alone.

The evening and the morning were the third day.

The Pyrenees from 'Episcopatus Balabastrensis et comitatus Ribagorcae' (1850)

4

Yr hwn yn unig sydd yn taenu y nefoedd, ac yn sathru ar donnau y môr. Yr hwn sydd yn gwneuthur Arcturus, Orion, a Phleiades, ac ystafelloedd y deau. Yr hwn sydd yn gwneuthur pethau mawrion anchwiliadwy, a rhyfeddodau aneirif.

Who alone stretched out the heavens and trampled the waves of the sea; who made the Bear and Orion, the Pleiades and the chambers of the south; who does great things beyond searching out, and marvellous things beyond number.

Extract from Job 9

The stars are out. We play with them on the vast game-board of the sky. Whose move is it now? The seasons move the counters because it is a long game which takes a lifetime to complete. The counters are out of reach and I realise that we are merely watching the game, living our lives under a thousand pieces. The constellations are different in the Pyrenees. Orion is called Solomon the Hunter.[12] He can be seen with his dogs chasing a hare across the night sky. As it turns out, that hare is the devil and the shepherds are safe once the hunt is over. The sun comes out. He is the same here. We try and look at him but our eyes cannot bear the light.

12 See Legend 'King Solomon'. As told by Dominica Giltzu, from Zugarramurdi, in 1941.

I slept quite badly in Estós. Morning began with temporary amnesia; I had completely forgotten where I was. The sound of the door opening and the sudden yellow light illuminating the room disturbed and distorted my sense of what was real and what was simply another relic left over from my dreams. The door shut again and we were plunged back into darkness.

'Dad,' I was completely disorientated, 'there's a little boy sneaking around. He's trying to nick our stuff!'

'Where?'

'There!' Dad shuffled to the edge of the bed to see what it was.

'That's not a little boy you fool,' he was more awake than I was. 'That's the woman from last night. She probably went to the toilet or something.'

'Oh… sorry… she looks like a little boy though.'

'Shshsh! She can hear you.'

'Oh!'

From the second bunk she looked tiny and I must have been paranoid about losing my gear or I had dreamt about robbery. I always dream about being robbed. Usually I am returning home and my nice cello is gone or my bookshelves are empty. We soon laughed and the French people weren't amused. My dreams are always like this in the mountains.

I remember a couple of years ago we were staying near Gavarnie after a week of climbing. The hotel was

old and full of stuff. In the corridor there was a life-size
model of a French waiter holding a plate; it creeped me
out. The room was better. Under the small balcony –
which most places have in France – there was a waterfall
which entered a hole in the ground. After a good meal,
I fell into a deep sleep and found I was standing in a
long Catholic procession. This was very unfamiliar to
me. I looked around and saw a host of cripples and
devout pilgrims ascending a long stairway up to a cave.
It was very dark and the moon was unnaturally big.
I decided that this must have been Lourdes although
I had never actually been there and yet we weren't a
hundred miles away. The chanting was mixed with
smells, bells and a thousand candles lighting the way
like a galaxy. I eventually reached the mouth of the
cave and the Pope stood there blessing each entrant
with holy water. I could almost feel the drops on my
forehead. Inside the cave, the statues were unclear in
the dim distance. All I could see were the white eyes
of the virgin, a Christmas tree of candles, and an ivy
beard, dark green, surrounding the darkened statue
like a frame. That's when I realised I was on my knees
slowly creeping towards an altar-like place. When I got
there I stared at the man next to me. He was bald and
was dressed like an ancient:

'*Fy enw i yw Paul*,' (My name is Paul) he said.
At first I thought nothing of it. But he waited for a
response. This is the bit when one usually wakes up

but I wasn't waking up. I was waiting for a gunshot, a pinch, a feeling of utter devastation, disappointment or excitement. But there was nothing except for this figure waiting for a response.

'Paul?'

'*Ie. Fy enw i yw Paul.*' That's when it triggered. I must have psychologically placed one of my favourite characters in the dream. Or it might even have been a piece of undigested cheese or gravy like Scrooge? I laughed in my sleep and realised that it was being transmitted into this wonderland. He didn't laugh. He looked around in a confused way and then at me again. He was so familiar and I don't know why.

'*Paid!*' (Don't). This was getting stranger and stranger. I stopped laughing. His voice had a commanding and grave tone to it.

'*Paid beth?*' (Don't what?) I was so confused and baffled. It suddenly dawned on me that this wasn't just the Apostle Paul but he was also speaking in Welsh.

'*Paid dod i Lourdes!*' (Don't come to Lourdes!) There was determination in every word. When he finished, he got up without crossing himself and walked away. I was left in the darkness of the cave. The virgin was still there. I woke up sweating all over. Dad asked me, nearly straight away, whether I wanted to visit Lourdes or Tarbes that day. I didn't think for very long. Lourdes was a big no but looking back, I wonder if anything would have really happened if we'd gone there? Nothing probably, but some old remnant of rural superstition kept me from going there. Perhaps the mountains play with our dreams or the solitude causes us to remember what we actually dream about.

The toilets in Estós were outside. You had to walk around a herd of cows just to brush your teeth. Dad had chosen to brush his while al fresco. All I could see was a tall man, in the midst of cows, with a mouth full of foam; it all looked quite funny. He kept calling: 'There's a good cow, nice cow,' but with that voice one makes when playing chubby bunnies with marshmallows. I laughed to myself. On my way I noticed a faint, black inscription on a small white door. It said: '*La ducha*' which meant that there was probably a shower inside. *Sésame, ouvre-toi*; I was right. The taps looked old, but as I turned them, there was a clunky bang before a couple of drips hissed into hot water. To my delight, there was also a convenient bottle of mini shower gel which had been left by another pilgrim. Inside that cave-like place, I watched a spider making its web as I washed. He was trying and trying, but the heavy droplets made his life very difficult. Eventually, he attached a silken thread to the shower wall and I was glad for him. I hurriedly dried and opened the wooden door which revealed the magnificent home the spider had built for himself.

The sun was bright, young and powerful that

morning – the cows joined in with the birds' matins – they were definitely worshipping something. Everything is so sensuous in nature; this is the same with the natural religion that people are drawn to. So many religions simply ascend because it feels right. People feel like they ought to climb mountains to atone for their sins. As in the story of Sisyphus, man's life is that constant struggle to shift blame, sin, guilt, and shame up some hill. But the hill never ends and the peak gets higher and higher. They come up to the hills again and again with a nebular comment such as 'well, that was spiritual' and carry on with their day to day lives. Sometimes, they tie flags or wash themselves in holy streams. They do it again and again… It must be exhausting. Why does the pilgrim go up and down, up and down the same holy hill when he can never really pay for his wrong-doings? My faith is directed at a person who climbed a hill once and for all. His climb finished a work which I could never achieve. I'd rather enjoy these mountains knowing that all is done and paid for, rather than having to cart my sin up every hill I climb.

~

Mount Golgotha

Jerusalem feels darker than usual. The place they call Golgotha is occupied by three wooden crosses where three naked bodies have been lifted up on this Judean hill. A breathless Son starts talking to his Father:

'Father, forgive them, for they do not know what they do!'

A priest spits at the foot of the cross whilst some of the soldiers are shaking dice in a beaker; they're gambling for the carpenter's robe. Some of the religious people start shouting:

'He saved others; let Him save Himself if He is the Christ, the chosen of God!'

'Yes if you are the Christ,' one of the thieves starts addressing the carpenter, 'save yourself and us!'

'Quiet, Gestas! Do you not even fear God, seeing you are under the same condemnation? And we indeed justly, for we receive what we deserve; but this Man has done nothing wrong.'

Then he turned to Jesus.

'Lord, remember me when You come into Your Kingdom.'

Jesus breathes heavily before saying:

'Today, you will be with me in Paradise.'

The penitent thief slowly slips into the next life but the one in the middle is still held between heaven and earth; his cross is wedged in a rocky cairn. He sees his mother and comforts her. He sees his friend Ioan, and he sees so many angry faces in the background. It was about the sixth hour and a strange darkness covered the whole earth. The creaking wood frames the sounds of whimpering women whilst '*Eloi, Eloi, lama sabachthani*?' which is translated 'My God, my God, why hast thou forsaken me?' This great shout which leads into that great silence.

A soldier climbs the peak and lunges his spear into the side of the crucified one.

Another soldier cannot blink.

The earth shakes as the carpenter breathes a finished work.

Based on the gospel accounts of the crucifixion

~

We left Estós as soon as we could. The close proximity of the star warms you up and it is far easier to get burnt. Our coats protected our arms but our faces started suffering. Our skin started flaking like melted feathers; we were pink, and rapidly on our way to *bien cuit* in this Spanish kiln. If Bruegel was about he'd paint the landscape and leave out everything else. The mountains carry on. They don't need us. He'd paint the cliff, the rolling stones, the creeping heather, the wandering salamander and he might even include the vultures. But the cairns, the mountaineers and the paths would be eradicated from the scene.

Our journey took us west towards the Porte de Puerto Christo where we would climb Pic des Anes Cruzes before heading down towards Viados. The path was good but it was full of cowpats. Dodging these mounds eventually proves impossible and one must embrace the squelching terrain. The cows watch you. I always thought that their eyes looked like our eyes. Some of them had pointed horns and the little ones stayed close to their mothers. The mothers were adorned with large alpine bells that rang out together in this earliest form of campanology. Each field is its own campanile and the mountains provide amplification. Eventually we climbed higher than the pasture and the bells fade before disappearing altogether.

The Porte de Puerto Christo was beautiful and well worth the climb. A single cow fed on the path. She looked shyer than the others and she had cottoned on that there might be better pasture over the col but she was well-disciplined and stopped before the next valley. Perhaps it was Baratxuri or 'Little Garlic', who fell asleep after taken her cows out to graze.[13] One cow mistook her for a blade of grass and swallowed her whole. When she saw that the cows did not return home, the mother feared that some accident had befallen Baratxuri and she ran out in search of her.

13 See story 'Baratxuri'. Recorded by Francisco de Etxeberria, from Andoain, in 1925.

When she arrived at the place where the cows were grazing, the mother started hollering Baratxuri's name, when the girl answered,

'Here I am!' The mother could hear her but could not see her.

'Where are you?'

'I'm in the stomach, look.' The mother saw a small little fist start beating from the cow's inside like a drummer's stick. The mother gathered the cows and drove them home. When the time was right, Baratxuri left the stomach in the usual manner. It took many days to eradicate the smell. I always liked that story. The same girl would have adventures travelling in a *burro*'s ear, but that's another story.

I patted one of the cows and carried on. Even animals seem to have their borders and they know when they have gone too far. To me, the name of this place sounded as if it were the door to Christ's Port. I was probably completely wrong but before I could look up its definition I re-drew my father and imagined that he was now the cartographer that named this place one star-lit night. The beauty overwhelmed him and made him religious all over again. For some reason, he started thinking about the Second Coming and his Michelangelo eyes saw *Kixmi* coming on a cloudy ship. The cartographer decided that this would be his landing place. The stars are like buoys in the black sea – a sea that separates time and eternity. The captain will follow each star like a glowing cairn, one after the other, when he journeys back to earth. The stars were brightest in this place which meant that the Porte de Puerto Christo was probably the spot where he might come ashore. The peaks would bow down and create a jetty in the air whilst all the storms would retreat as their master approaches. The wind would stop and the birds would float like seahorses in the deepest oceans. I could have looked for the real definition of this place but I decided against it.

My father sleeping on the Porte

My father was about fifteen minutes behind me. His *burro*-like pace meant that there was something wrong. A grey head appeared over the crest and he declared that he was ill as well.

'I don't feel well.'

'What's wrong?'

'Just give me five, will you.'

'Okay.'

We stopped for a bit; five minutes turned into an hour. I looked around. There was a small path on our right which looked as if it were heading up towards a peak. That was where we were going and it seemed a bit dubious. Watching my father sleep was a strange experience. I could see an older me lying there or even another Placidus a Spescha in his North Face cowl.

So begins the Peak des Anes Cruzes. Dad got up after his nap and said 'Come on then' as if nothing had happened. The first section of the climb was flat and grassy. The views were spectacular and the wind wasn't too bad either. I started thinking about Hemingway again. We hadn't seen him for a couple of days but he was still on our minds. Every time we looked at the map, we thought about his progress. His appearance had been so brief but it had had such an effect on both of us that he constantly came up in our conversation and thoughts. Something inside me said that we would meet him again. I wanted to know more about him, especially after hearing the tragic story about Manon.

There was something mystical about a grieving traveller crossing a mountain range after so much suffering. The mountains provide an escape for those who suffer. Each white hill is Narnian at first sight and when you descend into the real world again it's like stepping out of the Pevensie wardrobe. The difference is that life does change and people come and go like migrating birds. It's a myth that time stops because the clock continues on the slopes even though it is harder to hear each chime the hour makes. The bells still ring and our steps gradually become slower. There comes a time when the hill will be very difficult to climb and the riddle of the Sphinx will enfold before our eyes. But maybe I will need two sticks rather than one. The peaks will be higher and my hair will be the colour of the clouds.

'He was a mystical character wasn't he?' I was musing.

'What do you mean?' Dad asked.

'Well, he just opened up, you know.'

'I suppose. He seems to be looking for something up here.'

'God, or—?'

'Maybe. I should think he's fed up of all the noise. It's hard to hear yourself, let alone God, when there's so much noise.'

'Very philosophical, Pa,' I poke him with my stick, 'but I think you're right.'

We left our rucksacks in a place where the rock curled over the grass, creating a natural wave, frozen before it hit the ground. Nobody would steal them anyway because there was nobody nearby. The marmots might have stolen some food but I secretly hoped that they would because I wanted to encounter them again. When climbing, you need to be as light as you can. A heavy bag knocks you off balance and it can make you fall. There's nothing worse than being off balance on a knife-edge ridge. Being near the rock is vital and you know you are close enough to the cliff when your breath starts bouncing back at you. These are the times when your bag must not drag you away from the rock face. If it does, you might fall, and many have fallen with their burdens still strapped on.

'I was with your grandfather once on the Isle of Skye.' Dad does this. He randomly starts a completely different conversation or story.

'Oh?' I responded.

'Yes. We were on Skye climbing the *Cuillins*. You know how Grandpa walks.' In my head I conjured up my English grandfather.

'Yes.'

'And you know how he falls?' In my head I conjured up an image of my grandfather doing an S.T. Coleridge and just walking off a cliff or cycling off a promenade.

'Yes.'

'Well he fell, and mercy, I thought I'd lost the poor

fellow. He just slipped on this slab and continued over the edge like a rag doll. I thought that was it. I thought he was gone.'

'Well what happened?'

'I found him further down the hill with a dislocated shoulder.'

'Crumbs.'

As he finished his chronicle, the grass disappeared and we stepped on to the worst kind of scree called a church roof. The accumulation of rock debris becomes very inconvenient for a heavy climber. Each step was an extra effort and if it hadn't been for my stick I would definitely have been on all fours. It reminded me of Corris in north Wales where the slate mounds are similar in composition. As a child, I tried running up one of those mounds. It ended up being a futile exercise because I fell and a piece of sharp slate pierced my palm. There is still a mark on my hand where north Wales entered my skin.

When I think of slate, my mind's eye sees my great-great-grandfather (on my mother's side) working in the slate quarries of Bethesda. He would have loved touching the air up here and grabbing the different types of rock. I was told how he used to swing from the quarry edge on a rope in order to plant dynamite.

The bugle would sound and the imminent
blast   cut the rock causing
big slices
        of slate
                to hurtle

                down

                to

                the

                quarry floor.

He was a climber though. His fingertips were hardened from the manual work and his body lean, muscular and lizard-like, would have made him a better rock climber than his larger descendant. They were too poor. The quarries are silent now and the workers have been decommissioned from our memories. After the final signal of the morning was sounded, and the blast had done its job, the workers would scramble towards the *caban* (cabin). They'd gather in the lunch hour to eat their lunch and drink tea. The men sat in strict order.

The youngest boys sat closest to the door and the more senior men nearer the stove which stood in the middle of the room. The *caban* also contained a *ffowntan* (the fountain); this is what the workers called the tea-urn that would be constantly simmering, ready to brew the lunchtime tea. In a way, these little square, corrugated iron roofed huts were similar to the shepherds' cabins in the Pyrenees. Inside, they had the necessary food and warmth but they also became little concentrated centres of culture. Poetry was churned out in these places. Verses were flavoured with religion, politics and the love of creation, which went well with that language which was nurtured in these square wombs. They sang their spirituals too; sweet chariots changed into the rhythms of *Aberystwyth*.

~

The Mount of Olives

His friends were sound asleep. He had asked them to pray but their eyes were heavier than lead. He returned to the grassy spot where his knees had marked the hillside. The dew fell with a light touch. His tears were heavy. The garden was situated on the slopes of Olivet. The place was still and the trees' branches looked like ancient fingers harvesting air for a subterranean world. They closed in on him. Across the valley, the noise of a modern city fused with lights, shouts, neighing horses and the opening and closing of gates. The air was saturated with prayers.

The torches were getting closer. His friends were gone. His Father slowly turned His back on him as the garden closed in. Even the birds fled to the rooftops in the city whilst the autumn arrived early. Creation started groaning in confusion as its instigator knelt in its garden. His sweat was bloody: 'O Father, if this cup will not pass away, except I drink it, thy will be done.'

The Mount of Olives never forgot this mountaineer.

Based on the account in Matthew 26

∼

The slate slope was changing as we stepped on it. Each step made holes or shifted large quantities of stone down the hill. At the time, this was scary for me. It's a good thing you can't see the future. A couple of years later I would be walking the Tour de l'Oisans around the Massif des Écrins which was much worse. Yes, those cols in the Écrins have foot-holes that wouldn't even fit your little sister's feet and they're definitely not ideal when you have massive feet and a big bag on your back. You sweat so much. Things get ten times worse when your leg starts shaking uncontrollably – drunk with fear. This happens a lot. I don't know if it's just me, I've never asked Dad. Maybe it's because I'm such a bad, or rather, 'unexperienced' climber. You look down and you realise that you can't stop it. It's very odd. It's so tense that I always imagine, probably in state of quasi madness, a troop of bass choristers singing my own requiem to me from the col. In these instances, I discovered that breathing is important. Deep breaths, your leg slows down, deep breath, it slows down even more, deep breath, the doom-singing choristers disappear, and I can then carry on. Climbers who say they're fearless are lying. Fear is inevitable and can be healthy. It sharpens the senses. Doubt can sometimes do the same thing. A believer without no doubt whatsoever is a bit suspect. I am always reminded of that man who came to Jesus for help because his son was very sick. Jesus said to him: 'If you can believe, all things are possible to him that believes.' The man answered with tears in his eyes: 'Lord I believe; help my unbelief!'

There was a shadow again. It was the vulture-like witch or was it the witch-like vulture? It was a bird because, for some reason, they are usually much more frightening. The vulture was closer this time which indicated our height gain. We touched the first cairn which indicated a minor peak and carried on along a ridge, each section looking like the top of Cologne Cathedral, with long drops on both sides. My father was confident and he changed into a chamois whilst I felt like a tortoise, giddy and awkward.

'Keep your body upright!' Dad shouts.

'Why?'

'You'll keep your balance. Keep walking. Come on.'

I was afraid but I did what I was told. We reached a good height but the ridge then made an 'L' shape. I managed the vertical bit of the 'L' but the horizontal bit was too much for me. I grabbed the rock in front of me with my hands and embraced the earth. I felt like Blake's picture of Nebuchadnezzar when the old Babylonian king has been turned into a beast. My hands became feet and there was fear in my eyes.

So, I did what I do best, and hid in the rock. As I hid, I looked around. Dad was moving further and further away.

'Wait here. I need to get closer to the peak.'

'Okay.'

At first I could make out his features bobbing up and down the rocky col like a vessel in a choppy sea. Slowly he changed into a dot. Eventually he looked like a point that a biro makes on paper. In Celtic mythology, we have this thing called the *Cannwyll Corff* or the corpse candle: it is meant to be an omen of death. It is believed that when a death is imminent or if someone has just died a light will appear on the horizon like a candle indicating that the soul has left or is about to leave the body. I trusted that Dad was fine but the two or three vultures circling over my head were not the most encouraging of omens. The distant red dot was a corpse candle; the birds added to this gathering of bad omens. I half expected a black cat to jump onto my lap, or to roll up my sleeve and see the number thirteen written on my wrist. It was the vultures that bothered me the most. They were wondering whether I had died and whether my movements were simply the twitches of a corpse. I have never again experienced being watched like that. Humans are usually the predators and when a scavenger starts circling you whilst you're still alive you feel threatened. I stood up and started waving my fist like a maniac. Why wouldn't they go? I could see their small heads checking me out and it wasn't until I started waving my red coat at them that they distanced themselves. I watched the dot as it progressed towards the peak.

~

Mount Moriah

'Father, where are we going?' a youth asks his mountaineering father. The slope is mossy but an old path has been carved into its side by a flock of sheep. His father's voice had been very cold that morning.

'Moriah.'

'What does it mean?

'Ordained by YAHWEH.'

The father holds a torch whilst his sacrificing knife is tucked into his belt. His beard is whiter than the clouds and his eyes are like the stars. The boy carries the wood knowing that they are about to offer a burnt offering.

'Father, we have the wood and the fire. Where's the lamb?'

The father doesn't answer for a while; he is haunted by the words that had passed between him and the Lord.

'*Jehovahjireh.*'[14]

It had been a long climb. Days had gone by. The boy finds it difficult. His family has always enjoyed the high places, especially his father. But today he seemed different. Usually, it was in these places that his father communicated with the stranger that his mother had told him about:

'It was Him that appeared to your father under the terebinth trees before you were born. He promised you to us. It was impossible. I laughed. I doubted it all. But your father believed. Before not too long, you were born. Sometimes your father wanders up the hills and comes back with a glowing face.'

But his face didn't glow today. Isaac looked around for the stranger that his imagination had conjured up but he could only see the sheep on the slopes.

14 Jehovahjireh (The Lord will see to it).

They arrive at the peak. 'Fetch those stones, my son.' Abraham starts placing stone upon stone and an altar begins to take shape. His hand touches his son's hand as they pass the stones to one another. He looks up now and again, before returning to the altar.

'The wood, Isaac.'

Isaac places the wood on the stones. There are no lambs nearby. The sheep are too high and the stranger is nowhere to be seen.

'Lie down.'

Isaac closes his eyes and feels the warmth of the wood. He understands. He lets his hands stretch out; he allows his feet to rest on top of each other; he touches the cold stones; he feels forsaken. And Abraham takes the knife. And looks up once more before lifting his hand for the strike.

'Abraham!' It is a strange voice. Isaac opens his eyes. There is a ram caught in the thicket.

Based on the account in Genesis 22

~

The vultures were gone at last but I still felt exposed on this high altar. Meanwhile, my father was slowly crawling towards the peak. After about an hour, I could see the dot heading up towards the last bit. I had failed, but reaching the final stone did not matter so much to me. The Italian climber Reinhold Messner (b.1944) would probably laugh if he saw me sitting in the rock. But I am not a great climber. By the time he was twenty-three, he was probably one of the best in Europe. I don't mind, because I still have my toes. He lost seven of his whilst climbing Nanga Parbat.

My father (a distant dot) reaching the Pic des Anes Cruzes

After Dad's return, we descended the long valley down to Refugio Viados (1760m). The paths were long and were cut into the hillside like little shelves for us to walk on. Every now and again we had to jump over small and large gaps because the streams had gradually battered through these human interventions. Ropes were provided on one section but sometimes your feet slipped anyway, especially if you were relying solely on the rope. We passed a dead sheep which stank, and then descended into the belly of the valley.

The valley slowly opened before us. It was lush and pastoral. Cue Beethoven's Sixth again. Unfortunately, the rain started as well, so the lush sixth symphony descended into the first notes of the fifth. The houses looked alpine. Some sheep were chilling in their pens, safe from the nasty vultures and cruel conditions of the upper hill. There were also a couple of dogs outside one house, zooming around the green like patrolling troopers. We got to the door and rang the little bell. This was a nice place. It reminded me of one of those warm, pinewood skiing chalets in the Swiss Alps.

Viados would have been a lovely place to stay. Unfortunately, we had to truncate our journey if we were going to get back into France within the seven days. The water that we drink high up is usually fine but even the old climbers used to mix wine with it just in case. Bad water can ruin a trip. We must have drunk some along the way. Anyway, we bought some *Naranja* and waved goodbye to the friendly gentlemen who did not charge us even for our late cancellation.

We decided that we would attempt to get a hotel room somewhere further into Spain. 'Typical!' I can hear you say it now: 'Hotel room! What a pair!' Well you've never experienced bad water in the hills have you? My advice to you is to use the Spanish hotels; they are usually cheaper than the hostels! Refuges, tents, bivouacs, hotels and auberges are all Pyrenean experiences and they all have their pros and cons. Some years we only use refuges; that means you don't have to carry so much food. Last year we carried tents and spent a couple of nights just in our sleeping bags when we were too tired to erect our canvases. The more remote you are; the more gear you need to carry. That's when refuges are vital. Food is what adds the pounds to your packs. The best thing is sleeping under the stars. Make sure you remember your hat though, otherwise you'll never fall asleep. The stars are magnificent. If you get a chance, find a remote spot in the hills. Clear the ground of any stones. Prepare your bivouac and look up. If you're an atheist or an agnostic before, you will need more faith after spending a proper night under the galaxies. You see, it takes a lot of faith to believe in nothing and you'll need more of it after experiencing the full glory of the heavens. You'll only see the full glory in the highest of places.

$\sim$

David's Mountain

A young shepherd watches his father's flocks near Bethlehem. He's had a rough day on the hills. A bear has already attacked some of his sheep and he has failed to get a fire going properly. He wraps some wool around his body and lies down on the earth.

He listens. The bells of his companions comfort him in the darkness. They jingle in harmony with the natural nocturne created by the wind and the cicadas. The sheep bleat thinking that David has gone. He stirs. They are happy again. He speaks to himself: 'The Lord has delivered me from the paw of the lion and the bear. He is my Shepherd'.[15]

He looks up. The stars are magnificent. 'The heavens declare the glory of God!' He slowly drifts into sleep, drunk on words and dampened by dew.

'David!' A man comes over the col. His shadow appears as a giant against the cliff.

'David!' It's one of his brothers.

'What is it?'

'Samuel, the prophet, has come to talk with you'.

The scene preceding 1 Samuel 16

~

---

15 1 Samuel 17:37 and Psalm 23:1.

We started walking along the road hoping that some car would pick us up and take us down to San Juan de Plan. The art of hitch-hiking is not an easy one to master. Chances are that you are more likely to be successful in an area like the Pyrenees because the people that drive around understand how crucial hitch-hiking is. Because most people have 4x4s in the mountains, they don't mind you getting in with muddy boots. It is better to separate. People are happier picking up one rather than two, especially when you're both men. For some reason, all the witches in the folktales are women. Today, all the dodgy hitch-hikers are men.

If you're trying to cross a border, don't bother hitch-hiking. I've only ever managed it twice. Once was kind of cheating because my friend and I used the BlaBlaCar app on my Iphone to get into Switzerland where there's no real border. But the second time, my father and I were climbing out of Andorra into France; we descended into the wrong valley while our refuge was on the other side. The long road from L'Hospitalet-près-l'Andorra up to the border is one that I know quite well. We spent over an hour and a half with our thumbs stretched out, avoiding juggernauts and the steady drizzle which makes life worse. We were giving up. The British cars zoomed by. The French cars sped up as they went by. The Spaniards didn't even see us. Lorries nearly killed us. A Scottish car passed by and started swearing at us with their middle fingers.

The motorbikes roared in laughter as they passed us. The Dutch had a good stare at us and the faithful Germans – who are usually the best for picking up hitch-hikers – were too worried about breaking any possible rules by aiding us across the border. We passed a flattened adder who'd had quite a painful death by the look of it; it was quite depressing, actually. In about fifty yards, we passed another dead creature which had lost all recognisable features. I then saw the tail which confirmed that it used to be a rabbit. Eventually, a car indicated. I was so happy. An Algerian couple drove us all the way and treated us like their own kin. Hitch-hiking is great when it works out.

My Dad and I walked on the road to San Juan for over four miles. The hard surface hurt our feet in our stiff mountain boots.

'Have I ever told you about my friend Vaughan?' Dad was in storytelling mode again.

'No, I don't think so.'

'Vaughan was a funny old boy. He was a Welshman and probably the greatest hitch-hiker I've ever known.'

Dad was smiling to himself, enjoying rationing his story of stories.

'Why was he the greatest?'

'Mhhm?' Dad was back in the eighties.

'Why was he the greatest hitch-hiker?'

'Oh... He went all the way from Aberystwyth to Afghanistan.'

'Get off!' I didn't expect that.

'Yes… lorries and cars… the whole way!' Dad was starting to sound Welsh.

'How do you know he got there?'

'Postcard.'

'Postcard?'

'Yes: a postcard from Kabul!'

'You're having me on.'

'No, honest. I'd met him through some of my climbing friends just after university.

He was a good climber. Wiry… thin… very light. He was a little bit older than the rest of us but he was always high as a kite. But he loved the hills and he was a jolly good hitch-hiker.'

'Postcard from Kabul?'

'Yes. I'll find it for you when I'm home. You couldn't do it now though, Nay-fun. It's hard enough flying there let alone hitch-hiking. It was easier in those days. I never heard from him after.'

Dad slipped back into a memory lane cake. I wouldn't be surprised if Vaughan was living somewhere on the slopes of a faraway hill. I can imagine him marrying a local shepherdess and hitch-hiking every day to get his groceries from a bazaar. Either that or he's probably dead. (Vaughan, wherever you are, if you're reading this, please let my father know whether you're still alive. Many thanks.) I started wondering whether Vaughan was Dad's Hemingway; his very own mystical mountain man who left an impression on a twenty-something climber from Thanet. Dad had been driven to the hills by the flatness of his hinterland. Thanet is one of the lesser known islands of the British Isles, partly because it isn't really an island anymore. Once upon a time, the island was separated from the mainland by the Wantsum Channel. Now it just looks like a drainage ditch. But the men of Kent are still proud of their island. By his late teens, my father had become fed up of being able to see a very long way. He longed for higher places. He, too, would hitch-hike up to Scotland where he spent many weeks of seven days.

The trees had grown huge and old by now. The road twisted down the hill like a snake in a tree. We followed it for a while until a random white van came into view.

'That's odd, isn't it, Dad?'

'Not really. It's probably hunters or foragers.'

'Look.'

Two short middle-aged women, backs bent, were lurking in the woodland. They carried baskets and had boots which would have looked look formidable on a seven foot warrior. We stopped to see what they were doing. Were they witches? We asked them and they answered in very good English:

'Picking mushrooms.' My father's eyes lit up. I suspect he'd known what they were up to all along but wanted to get tips from them about one of his own hobbies.

'What are you collecting?' My father asked the women.

'*Cèpe*,' they answered offering us some. They were good, despite looking like shrivelled-up dwarves' ears. *Cèpe* (*Boletus edulus*) is actually a generic term applying to several related species. I had recently read an article about the danger of mushroom picking on the continent. In some parts of France, the price of *Cèpe* can be as much as €70/kg, which has led to an increase in foraging. Tales of property owners chasing mushroom pickers from their land is very common. In the Gironde, one *gendarme* was injured whilst trying to cool down a farmer who was chasing mushroom pickers off his land with a spotlight and his 4x4. In Languedoc, one man crashed his getaway car whilst being pursued by three 'vicious landowners.' Poisoning happens now and again. People also get shot – mostly accidentally – *la chasse* (the French word for a hunt) has usually been going on (or so they say!). When I was growing up, Dad would bring big white mushrooms home from the fields. They always taste stronger than your usual Tesco button mushroom and are especially good grilled. The women gave us some more and wished us well. Unfortunately they did not offer us a lift. I think they had only just started foraging. With hindsight, I don't think they were witches.

The rain returned and we were forced to huddle under a few pathetic branches whilst waiting for a miraculous sight of headlamps. Would anyone come? The rain was so heavy that it started filling our boots and I imagined my dry clothes in the pack becoming sodden. A van came round the corner. I thumbed. He stopped. And I ran towards the sliding door of the VW camper. I opened it. I breathed a sigh of relief before being emotionally catapulted. I'd nearly put my hand into the gob of a savage dog!

I shouted. I looked at it whilst it barked at me; I was too scared to move. I noticed it only had three legs. Things like that never help.

'Dad, stay away, there's a savage dog!'

Dad came round the corner and stopped by my side.

'Oh yes it is rather large,' he then switched into his French which always cracks me up: 'Mercy mon-sir. Mercy boo-coo. It is okay, the woof woof, yes?'

The man had a big smile and he held his dog back, patting him on his head as if he were trying to convince us that the beast was actually more Chihuahua than Baskerville.

'He's a big softy and is actually little sick in the head if you know what I mean. Don't worry!' Well, you didn't need a PhD to see that, I can tell you.

'Yes he lost his leg.' You didn't need a PhD to see that either. We didn't ask about the leg but the driver felt compelled to keep talking. He held the dog back until my father and I were sitting 'comfortably' in his VW campervan. I was really 'grateful' but I was petrified of Cerberus.

'Yes he lost his leg somehow. One day he had four legs. The next day he come home with three legs. My girlfriend say: "My lovely, our *chien* seems to have lost his leg!" I come around the corner and poor Robespierre is finding it very, very difficult to stand up. Let alone walk! It had gone. What you say in England? Vanish, yes, phoo!'

Dad and I nodded as the man did the vanishing gesture with his hand.

'What do you do?' My father asked the driver. He thought he would break that unique ice of a situation where a child-eating dog is eyeing you up. As soon as Dad opened his mouth, the dog barked and barked. The man had started driving by now.

'I took him to the animal doctor.'

'No, I mean what is your occupation? Your work?'

'Pompier!' he shouted. The dog howled. 'Shut up Robespierre!' The driver re-adjusted his foot over the dog's lead. 'Don't worry about my dog. He is just a little scared of you people.'

The dog is scared, I thought, well that's ironic! He was definitely not scared and I reckon he would have bitten us if it wasn't for the Pompier's foot. And who calls their canine after the instigator of France's Reign of Terror anyway. Names are jolly important, you know, when it comes to character development.

'And you guys?' Robespierre barked even louder.

'I'm a student and my father is a lecturer,' I answered. The fireman took out a bag of pistachio nuts as a gift. I think he felt a bit bad about his bloodthirsty hound. He threw them to Dad who then handed me a couple. They were good. He also offered us a bottle of water each which we gladly accepted. The dog was growling and his saliva dribbled on the floor, drip by drip.

'Where you guys heading?'

'San Juan de Plan. Is that okay?'

'Yes, certainly. That is where I go too.' I don't think I blinked for the whole journey. I tried to look around to distract myself. The campervan was nicely kitted out for this one man and his three-legged dog. There was a couch for him and a basket for his Cavall. I re-named him Cavall, instead of Cerberus, after Arthur's hunting dog. In *De Mirabilibus Brittaniae*, the dog left his footprint in a rock whilst pursuing the *twrch trwyth*, a giant boar that ravaged Britain. The wondrous nature of this footprint was that if you removed the stone from the original heap where it lay and put it somewhere else, it would return to its original spot the next day. Perhaps that is why this Cavall has three legs. His determined nature wore one of his legs out and when he left an imprint his whole leg was left behind in the rock. This dog still looked as if he could chase a wild boar even with a missing leg. The van had red curtains over each window so the interior looked like a darkroom for developing photographs. If you'd taken a picture, you would have seen two men nibbling pistachio nuts and a large piece of dog probably taking up half the picture.

San Juan came into view. The little church was lit up by the moon because it was night by the time we got into the village. We found a very nice hotel for a good price and we enjoyed some *huevos rotos* before bed. It's never a good idea to eat before you sleep.

$\sim$

The Tale of Hemingway and the Lake

That night, I dreamt I was home again. I was no longer in San Juan with its campanile but I was walking in the Bannau of Carmarthen. I could feel the snow on my cheeks and the memories of previous walks had fused into one painted scene. The sheep were studded randomly across the hills and the folds of the sleeping lords led me up to the peat bogs which squelched as I stepped on that damp carpet.[16] I walked towards the small fishery where fairy-like trout leapt up in salutation. I waved my hand and the fish became flying fish which flew to other rivers out of sight. And then I saw him. Picws Du. My mountain.

---

16 The Sleeping Lord - In Arthurian myth, this refers to rex quondam rexque futurus (king once, king to be). A mythical sleeper who is sometimes an analogue to Christ.

I arrived at the magical lake at the foot of Picws, Llyn y Fan Fach. I sat there in a kind of in-dream reverie and watched the waves bob up and down in the moonlight. I felt so lonely. As I watched the water, a lonely climber was coming down the hill. At first, he looked like a man in a grey cloak. I had somehow acquired night-vision and I looked into the lake and my eyes were sparkling. I looked up again and the climber was getting closer and had taken his grey cloak and rolled it under his arms. His hat was pulled over half his face. His shorts were stained with coffee marks; sleeves rolled up; a huge pack; a staff in one hand and a ski pole in the other whilst he hobbled down with the robe in his armpit.

I looked at the lake again and on the opposite bank there was a young woman sitting on the shore. I got up and hid in a hole in the peat. I looked up again at the mountaineer and I recognised his face: it was Hemingway.

The moon moved slowly over the peak. Was she *Wislogee?*[17] Or Manon? Could she be another witch? I had no idea. Hemingway and the girl came face to face. I got as close as I could and made out some words:

'Excuse me, I thought you were somebody else,' said Hemingway.

'I am sorry. I am waiting for a younger man. If it is you, then some enchantment has aged you overnight?

17 Wislogee - The Breton name for Guinevere meaning 'white and joyous'.

Or could you be *Ambrosius?*[18] She laughed.

'Forgive me, Lady, I am merely a pilgrim.'

'God speed to you.'

'And to you.'

The old man girded himself and carried on, leaving the woman by the lake. As he walked, he saw a local boy coming with bread wrapped in a tea-cloth. His hair was blacker than the night and his eyes were whiter than the moon. He passed Hemingway and they both nodded at one another as if the whole scene had been choreographed. Hemingway turned round again and slowly veered towards the trench where I was hiding. The boy stayed by the lake, hand-in-hand with his beloved.

'Psst!' I tried to get his attention. He looked around thinking that his tinnitus had returned.

'Psst!' He looked again and saw me with my finger over my mouth. He completely ignored my advice: 'Aaaahhh! Long time no see, no?!'

'Shshsh! They'll hear. We better move back or they'll see us.' Hemingway looked confused.

'Why are you watching, *mon ami*?'

'Why are you watching?'

'I feel there is something weird about all of this! Some enchantment I think?'

'Ditto.'

'Good.' He noticed that my eyes were glittering. 'What has happened to your eyes?'

18 Ambrosius - Another name for Emrys, Myrddin or Merlin.

He laughed.

'I don't know… keep it down… look something's happening!'

We huddled closer to one another and noticed that the girl was gone.

'Where did she go?' I asked.

'I don't know, maybe she got away?'

'Look!'

The water of the lake began to boil. I nudged Hemingway and we watched as the girl re-appeared, accompanied by two figures from the deep. One was an old man with pond weed in his hair. His body was that of a young man's but his face was old and his beard long. He must have been her father. The other one looked like her twin sister. After gazing for a minute or two we realised that they were identical.

'I can't hear anything!' I said.

'Nor me. It feels as if I've got water in my ears. There is something fishy going on here!'

This annoyed us both. We wanted to hear what was going on. The young man was obviously facing some test but we couldn't hear anything. It looked like he was studying them both. He pointed at one of them. The old man smiled and turned back into the water. It was obvious that the boy had passed the test and had recognised the girl that he was in love with.

'*Mon Dieu*! Very strange indeed. Good for him! I wonder how did they manage to breathe down there?'

I looked at Hemingway and we both shrugged our shoulders at the same time. The second girl faded away and left the original couple together. What happened next was stranger still.

'Look, the water!' Hemingway got up, forgetting that we were meant to be incognito. The water bubbled like a cauldron. Then a duck came up from the deep.

'Haha, *mon ami*, look, a duck!' Hemingway was enjoying the whole scene. As he laughed the water bubbled and bubbled producing more ducks, sheep, geese, pigs, three cats, cows, a bull, some horses, chickens, goats, a cockerel and a sheepdog, came bleating, mooing, cooing and so forth out from the water. They looked as healthy as any other farm animal even though they'd come from underwater. All the animals followed the boy and girl towards the village of Myddfai. I looked at Hemingway and he looked at me. And in a moment or two, everything was quiet.

Hemingway opened his sack and lifted some logs, kindling, and a box of matches from its mouth. I looked up. The moon hovered over Picws and illuminated its face. Hemingway started a fire. The flames licked the air and hissed as the snow dropped to its core.

'That was very strange, no?!'

'Yes it was strange.'

I laid back in my dream, and counted the stars that were like rivets hammered into the black shield of the sky. As I was about to wake, I saw something even more wonderful on the peak. A man was watching us from the ridge. He was sitting on a white stag.

Based on several myths based around Llyn y Fan Fach in Carmarthenshire. I grew up in this area.

~

I woke up. My body was back in San Juan but my soul was still staring up at Picws Du. It was a perfect night outside. The hills in the distance were watching us. They seemed to be surprised that we had left so soon. I realised that Hemingway was probably up there somewhere opening his sack and lifting some logs, kindling, and a box of matches from its mouth. He was probably warming his big hands whilst cooking his soup. His favourite dish was soup with pieces of *saucisse* warmed up in its broth. He'd be sleeping before long. Dad was snoring on the other side of the room. I wondered whether he was in Carmarthenshire. I doubt it. He was probably walking some Scottish Munro. Maybe he was chatting with Ossian or simply wandering towards a lonely bothy in a heather sea.

The evening and the morning were the fourth day.

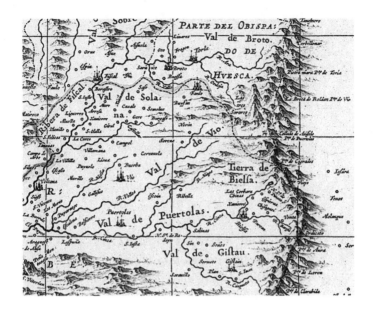

Bielsa Map

5

¿Por qué, decidme, hacia los altos llanos
huye mi corazón de esta ribera,
y en esta tierra labradora y marinera
suspiro por los yermos Castellanos?

Tell me, why does my heart run
from the fertile fields and the cool shores of
the lowlands? Why does it long for barren
Castilian uplands? Tell me.

Los Sueños dialogados', Antonio Machado

Silver streaks swim in the streams. Sometimes it is just light, but at other times these flashes indicate that fish are flowing around the rocks. I see their little mouths surfacing for a quick snack or a shot of air. Man writes his advertisements whilst whipping monofilament line; this is an irresistible language for the fish. The line speaks of a starry galaxy where flies are abundant and where the fish can view their world from another space. My heart longs for the uplands too. I climb its many faces where things like fish pass into mythology. In Wales, there is a place where they rode on a salmon's back because he had grown so big with age. In these uplands, the water threads its way through the dusty channels of stone and the fish might be growing bigger at the bottom of some undisturbed pool.

San Juan was our alarm clock. The noise of life was unbearable at the beginning, with the sudden acceleration of a van, the jabber of the local postman and barking dogs. Bells soothed us but the cooing woodpigeon invited us to return to the uplands. Dad was stuffing his things into his rucksack. This had become a ritual. The clothes were wrapped in a bin bag, then the food, then his big First Aid box (which could have done with its own porter). Dad is a hypochondriac. But then, I suppose, so am I.

'You got everything?'

'Yes.'

'You're sure?'

'Yes.'

'Check under the beds.'

'I have.'

'Okay.'

We began by going into the local *supermercado* where we re-stocked on our Fanta *Naranja*. We filled our *Sigg* bottles with ambrosia before San Juan waved farewell with the sounding of its bell. A hundred yards and we had to stop.

'Stop!' Dad cried,

'What now?'

'Fizzing. Your bottle's fizzing.'

Note to self and to all. Fanta is fizzy. When walking, it will fizz and make your rucksack sticky. Thankfully, our clothes were in bin bags.

We spent most of this fifth day hitch-hiking back into France. We walked for about a mile when a guy picked us up in his blue car. His name was Alejandro and after a difficult beginning we finally understood that he owned a rafting business in Salinas. He was not very talkative but he did drive his car like an artist. Each turn was like a stroke of a brush, painting the road at a good, fun speed. I can remember thinking that 'crossing borders is not all that difficult. If we could get a couple of lifts like this we'd be over in no time.' The road from Plan went all the way to a crossroads at Salinas. If you turned left, you would go further into Spain. Our road, the road uphill, snaked up towards Bielsa before eventually reaching the Tunnel d'Aragnouet and our passage back into France. But that was a long way off and we would have to get a lift through the tunnel because walking through is not allowed.

As Alejandro drove us down the hill, I thought about the Spanish poet Antonio Machado (1875-1939) and how he had been forced across the French/Spanish border in 1939. Both Antonio, his mother, and the rest of the defeated Republican army crossed near the French town of Collioure. The weather was against them from the beginning and they did not even have a *burro*; they crossed on foot in icy rain. Both he and his mother died soon after crossing. After his death, they found a crumpled-up piece of paper in his overcoat pocket. It was one line and it read: *Estos días azules y este sol de infancia* (These blue days and this sun of childhood). The Fascists had driven him higher and higher. They'd driven him out of his Castilian uplands and tried to shut the poet up. The sky might have been dark above Barcelona and the memories of Guernica made it greyer and greyer until even the cows seemed to vomit in fear. The Catalan language was suppressed and the Spanish stamp was stuck over the fissiparous colour of Pyrenean identity. War crimes were committed and the mountains either delivered one or passed a death sentence, depending where and when you chose to cross. Somehow, Machado saw blue skies again and the sun of childhood started shining again.

We were dropped off at Salinas de Bielsa and we started walking uphill again. Lorries hurtled past as if we weren't even there. Dad enjoys a personal dual with drivers as he walks:

'This is ridiculous. Slow down… You idiot!'

'They can't hear you, mind,' a wing mirror nearly decapitated him.

'Idiot! Moron! Stupid fool!' Think Hergé's Captain Haddock minus the beard and you're there. He stopped. He put down his sack. He pulls his stick out. He makes a stance of 90° with the stick going straight out into the road from his hip.

'Ha! That'll stop the Neanderthals. It's 'cos we're British.'

'Welsh.'

'Ha!'

Going along a road can be either very boring or very fascinating. It's amazing what we saw. Bottles, chocolate wrappers, dummies, a shoe, an old umbrella and a pornographic magazine; all this made the odd roadkill look a bit tame. I felt like going up and down with a leper's bell pronouncing this highway 'Unclean!' But there were flowers, and we found an old glass bottle that Dad added to his collection.

Now and again, we passed abandoned houses. For some reason, the town of Dunwich came into my mind. Dunwich was a rotten borough which sent MPs to Parliament even though most of the formerly prosperous town had fallen into the sea. I wonder if anyone still represented this Pyrenean Dunwich. An abandoned house does not have to go that way, of course. In *The Shipping News*, the old Quoyle house was dragged across the sea-ice to its new position somewhere on the Newfoundland coast. It was then cabled to the ground at the four corners in order to stop it from being blown away. Perhaps if the locals had dragged these houses further from the edge and cabled them down they might still be habitable. But the city was an easier option. Cities can be bad because you can lose that intimacy that our forefathers had with their land. In Welsh, this beloved patch is called the *milltir sgwâr* (square mile), a space that defined and created who you were. No wonder families became known by the names of their villages or their farmhouses especially, when so many of them shared the same surname.

I looked through one of the windows and saw an old candleholder rusting on a stone floor whilst a drip-drip came through a hole in the roof. There was a tree growing in the corner and the discarded wardrobe of pigeons was just thrown on the floor. Dad had entered the abandoned house and was prodding around. He was looking for goodies. 'Nothing here. Let's go. Farewell cooing Lords.' I nodded at the birds before continuing up the road.

It wasn't too long before another car pulled up beside us. It was a dark red Volvo driven by an old fruit-seller who was smoking a cigar. I entered with about six or seven 'Gracias', breathing in the incense, and preparing myself for the next leg of the journey.

'Where you from?' the old man asked, struggling to take the Volvo from second to third gear.

'*Gales*,' we answered. He'd obviously heard about Wales or he was just being polite.

'And you?' My father asked.

'Bielsa', I recognised the town from the map. 'You walk long way?' he continued.

'*Sí*. We've walked from *Francia*,' my father answered.

The man nodded and went on to say how he had climbed most of the principal peaks as a youth. He puffed his cigar and happily drove at about 25 miles an hour up the hill through Bielsa itself. He started babbling something in Spanish about the church and I wished I'd paid more attention in school. For some strange reason, my school taught French one week and then Spanish the following week and so on, which made for a very confusing linguistic education. I decided to focus on French, and now, I regret not making the most of four languages that were presented to me at such a young age.

The old man changed back into English and as we drove through Bielsa he gave us a quick history of the town. Like Guernica, Bielsa had been completely destroyed during the Spanish Civil War. I noticed that all the houses looked relatively new and that there was a sense of recovery still residing in the air. It takes a lifetime to get over a war, the sounds never leave the trees and the bloodstains are never washed away. He then told us about the *Trangas*:

'What's *Trangas*?'

'It's a festival,' he answered.

'Celebrating what?' I asked.

'The purpose is to say goodbye to winter and greet the arrival of spring.'

'What happens during this festival?' Dad continued,

'The men wear big ram's horns on their heads. They

also make their faces all black and use potatoes as fake teeth. It is very good and it represents fertility.' He nodded as I drew some ram's horns on his head, trying to imagine him during *Trangas*.

Trangas en carnival | 1950

I later found an old photograph with four barbarian-looking men holding their staffs. The Volvo driver would have been a teenager when these men were blackening their faces. Maybe his father is there or maybe his mother is taking the photograph. Our own ghostly midnight horses and men dressed like Biblical women do not seem all that strange when you hear about *Trangas*. In the Welsh valleys, we had the Scotch Cattle who were operating as late as 1926. The 'herd' would be led by a 'bull' who led the miners to the homes of those who worked during the strikes. Violence followed. The *Trangas* sounds older. This was a remnant of those Aralar dancers who spied the luminous cloud. The memory of those naked pagans seemed to live on in this old cigar-smoking man. *Kixmi* was now a crucified effigy in a dark, run-down church. Perhaps the men of Bielsa could not understand why He had allowed the events of the 1930s. He is far up the mountain again and these people have built their golden calves, re-erected the old altars and turned their backs on a dying idol. The dancers of Aralar have returned, and this time, they are wearing the horns of their sacrificed flocks.

The car rolled into Parzan. We thanked the old pagan before stretching out our thumbs again. Fortunately, this was a road of Good Samaritans, unlike in Britain where everyone passes you by. When I went walking in north Wales, my friends and I hitch-hiked most days. One weekend, we hitch-hiked five times. Four out of those five times we were picked up by Germans. My own people passed me by! The same thing happened outside Parzan. An old, small, red Volkswagen Golf pulled up. We looked inside the car and two German students gave us warm smiles. The girl almost embraced us and the boy grinned happily in a Panama hat and shades that were too small for his rectangle face. They told us to get in but it looked impossible. The back seats were a market stall: a picnic, three bottles of wine, clothes, souvenirs and a couple of baguettes. We eventually squeezed in and they struggled to start the car with the weight in the back. They introduced themselves as Gunther and Klara, literature students that cherished every single encounter in these mountains. Every person you meet might be Ernest Hemingway, and if it isn't, it does not matter because most humans have at least one Odyssey to talk about. They were celebrating her viva and they were thrilled that they had met an Englishman and his Welsh son on the French/Spanish border.

The golf went up the hill like a tractor but we eventually made it. I watched her soft hands hold his before he let go suddenly to change gear. Conversation went from the European Union, to the Welsh language, to a dialect that the boy's old grandmother spoke. I cannot remember which one. We are all brought up so differently and our languages are as varied as the fish in the sea but in these places, all are drawn to this rocky reef. These interruptions in the landscape draw the most colourful creatures. Some big fish swim nearby, but even us small fishes can get into the nooks and crannies and then hitch-hike on the backs of big whales.

We entered the tunnel and failed to hold our breaths whilst passing through one side of the reef to the other. It goes on for quite a while and the flashing lights lead us like buoys to the other side.

We were back in France and the D173 took us down from the hole in the hill to the main road in the valley. The golf picked up speed and I started settling in to the couch of rucksacks, wine bottles and baguettes before the sign for Saint-Lary-Soulan came into view. Our plan was to eat something in Saint Lary before heading back on the GR10 towards the villages of Azet and Germ before heading to the place where it all began. We said goodbye to our German friends – they were returning to Berlin for a family event.

~

Mount Ararat

Noah opens the door slowly. The land is scarred and re-made. A tree or two starts blossoming and Noah is overwhelmed by the solitude. Even the ground is empty. All the insects are behind them. The sky is so blue.

'What is it like, Father?' Shem asks,

'Quiet. Listen.' He whispers. The sons are fearful lest their breath should disturb the sanctity of the moment.

'Not for long,' Ham points as two snow leopards sneak their way between the family's legs as they stand in the doorway.

Noah follows them on to the land. The leopards seem

lost and they look up. God sees them and answers with a small dusting of snow. The leopards disappear. Noah is moved but walks away lest his sons should see. The ground crunches beneath him as his feet cracks the unexpected shells on the ridge. He looks down and smiles. Pebbles and stones have been churned up by the deluge and the whole mountainside seems to be stained with the damp markings of saltwater. The seaside smell is strange up high. Seaweed covers the cairns and the old hill, on which the ark rests, doesn't look like a grand building or a ziggurat. Noah looks at the rock and its sheen resembles a freshly-finished sculpture. The rock has been split, carried, hammered, crushed and polished by water, lightning, wind, and rain. He walks on and drinks the fresh air. Noah looks back, like all other mountaineers, and surveys the different faces of the hill. He is overwhelmed and starts building a new cairn.

Based on the account recorded in Genesis 8

~

It was nice seeing the red and white marks again. Dad pointed to the first one:

'The GR10. I wonder where Hemingway is by now?'

'Yes I was just thinking that.'

The little path went up from Saint Lary and rapidly

gained height. Now and again, we saw figures of the Virgin Mary which made us think of Hemingway's story. She opened her porcelain arms to the walkers as they passed by but nobody seemed to notice her. It was a long climb and we headed further and further into sheep-pasture again. The buzzing noise of the electric wire was an indication that livestock were not far away. Dad asked me:

'Did I tell you about Grandpa and the wire?'

'No?'

'When I was your age, we were walking up a hill somewhere and we came to a dead end. Our way was blocked by an electric fence.' I saw what was coming, 'Grandpa then said, "Wait here son whilst I just hold it down for you." He walked over. Plonked his foot over the wire which was tight, you know... I started walking over and the wire flicked up and got him in his Johnson! I've never heard such a scream!'

My grandfathers' exploits deserve their place in the annals of our nation. One of them is a Welsh minister (Tadcu) and the other one is an English water-side character (Grandpa). Grandpa lives about thirty yards from the sea; he launches his boat most weeks, and keeps a loaded gun on top of the freezer. He's eighty years old and would be ready, if the time came, to cable down his house like a Quoyle.

'What's worse,' Dad continued, 'it happened again after I'd crossed over the fence. He swore ten times before lying on the grass in recovery mode.'

We laughed for a while. I was told that Grandpa had also climbed in the Pyrenees. He's very proud of the fact that he, and his rambling friends, conquered Canigou (2786m) one year. My other grandfather did something to his hip whilst climbing Pic D'Anie (2507m) in his sixties. Both grandfathers talk about their single peak in the Pyrenees. Maybe I'll be talking a lot about Spijeoles if I am blessed with grandchildren. What I do know is that I'm glad that my father and I didn't get caught on any fences.

The road slowly led us up to the village of Azet which is perched on the hillside. Its old houses hang on like a series of little nests on a green cliff. Perhaps the people feel nearer to the birds than their compatriots in the valley below. But Azet is not famous for its birds; the Azetois are famous for being sheep farmers although their coat of arms is actually sheep-less. There are two donkeys feeding on what looks like a Christmas tree; I like a good coat-of-arms! In the village, there is a very old church and a Pyrenean House of Pastoralism; both look deserted.

~

A Judean Hill

There are some *bergers* keeping their flocks on a Judean hill. Their flock seems unsettled and restless. These are temple sheep. A lot of lambs are needed for the feasts of Passover, Pentecost, Trumpets, and Tabernacles as well as on Yom Kippur, the great Day of Atonement.

It's colder than it usually is. The *bergers* aren't singing tonight. Their gaze thirsts for heat and their bodies are turned towards the flames.

'The sheep are strange tonight,' one of them says without blinking or even looking at the others.

'Yes… I've had a look around. I can't see why,' one of the others answers.

'Must be the cold.' They all nod at one another. The youngest one stretches for another piece of wood.

As he does so, the hillside turns eerily still. The fire dies. They're a bit frightened.

'What's going on?'

'I don't know.'

The moon shifts and the sky opens like a stage curtain. The brightest light they've ever seen shone above the peak. The rocks are suddenly slabs of silver and their eyes are glowing.

'Look!'

They cover their faces. The green hill is filled with the sweetest music. One of them dares to look through the gaps in his fingers. He sees a man standing nearby, backed by a deafening chorus of voices coming from an innumerable host of heavenly beings.

'Boys, look!' The shepherds open their eyes. The man smiles at them.

'Fear not!' he says.

'Who are you?' one of them asks.

'Are you the Messiah?' the youngest utters.

'No. I am a messenger. I have good news for you and for all. A Saviour has just been born in Bethlehem. He is the one you call Messiah – the Shepherd King. He will save his people from their sins.'

Silence.

The *bergers'* faces shine as the darkness returns. They look at one another. The sheep have fallen asleep.

'Come, let us go!' The youngest shepherd takes a sleeping lamb up into his arms and the others, some laughing, others crying, follow him down the mountain paths to the nearby settlement called Bethlehem.

Based on the account in Luke 2

~

Dad had quickened his pace and we'd separated for a brief time. As I entered Azet, I saw four old men sitting in a bus stop. Next to the stop was an old-fashioned streetlight mirroring the one that Lucy saw in Narnia. I knew I was in for a treat; there's nothing quite like a chat with our elders. They are usually more experienced in everything from romance and religion to the skills of comedy.

'*Bonjour,*' I approached, wearing my sky blue poncho, '*un homme dans un manteau rouge, um, passer ici?*'

I knew my father had passed by moments earlier, but I wanted the chance to speak to them. However, none of them said anything. They only smiled and pointed towards the house behind where I was standing. There was a white sign saying 'La Bergerie: Gite de Sejour.' This was the best place that I would stay that year.

The woman was very welcoming. Her name was Sylvie Guinet and she looked a bit like my Cornish aunty. An *auberge* is better than a refuge; I guess this was something between a refuge and a hotel. The difference was that at night-time she opened her front room to the locals where all and sundry would gather for food and pay at the end. I asked Sylvie about the men at the bus stop:

'Yes, they sit there every day, waiting,' she said with a grin on her face.

'What are they waiting for?' I asked.

'Once a day, a local farmer's daughter drives down the road and passes that bus stop in her white car. She is very beautiful and the men religiously sit there waiting for a sighting of her.' Perhaps her name was Rhiannon. In the *Mabinogi*, Rhiannon appears at Gorsedd Arberth riding a white horse where, Pwyll, the Prince of Dyfed, has been eagerly waiting for a sighting of her.

'Once she passes', our host continued, 'they all go home for their dinner! Can you believe it?! The cheek... and their poor wives!' She burst out laughing and shook her head in disbelief.

We spent most of the evening sitting in the dining room, listening to the sounds of the meal being prepared in the kitchen next door. This was definitely not mutton stew but real lamb, and lots of it – the smell confirmed this. My father studied the map and I was writing some notes when a large man silently walked through the door. It was a large man and it turned out to be none other than Monsieur Hemingway.

'*Mes amis gallois!*' He shouted with joy. We were so glad to see one another. He took our hands and sat us down.

'I must buy you some apple wine!' He called the host and ordered the drink. I whispered to Sylvie, 'Just tea please.' Hemingway never noticed. He had already started taking us through his journey, step by step, since we'd left d'Espingo.

'I became very ill and it take me many days to reach this spot. I only came from Germ this morning actually. The rain was so bad and my feet were hurting a lot.'

He took out the map and we spent an hour comparing our journeys. His was a straight line whilst ours was a kind of circuit.

'This place,' he points at the map, 'terrible. This place,' he points again, 'worse! This place,' Dad looks straight into his eyes 'what you British say, wonderfull. Yes, full of wonder. You know?' We both nodded. The meal was getting nearer and Hemingway shouted,

'*Mon cheri, l'odeur est le parfum*! Wonderful! No?!' He looked at us; we nodded.

The meal was excellent that evening. Big portions of lamb and dauphinoise potatoes have haunted my culinary dreams ever since. On the next table, there was a *berger* family with their new baby. Behind us, another family watched television whilst eating and we were on a table with Hemingway himself. As the night went on, a big, hot crème brûlée full of *cassis* arrived and with each spoonful, more and more people started to congregate in the main dining room. Some people tried to get in but it was so full. A couple knocked on the door. I looked through a gap in between all the people and I thought that the woman looked heavily pregnant. The man looked in a terrible state and he graciously bowed his head when Sylvie turned them away.

The stories and jokes started. One man said how some scoundrel had stolen all his hubcaps and he re-enacted how he openly cursed him on the street, gestures and all. The women talked about sheep and how it was a bad year. Another man was deep into mushroom talk whilst Hemingway seemed to drop in and out of everyone's conversation all at once. He was in his element. He called the host over and started telling her about Espingo and how her house was an excellent house compared to our first refuge:

'You should send your daughter or your son there. They can teach them how to cook!' The family was flattered by Hemingway's compliments and he praised everything from the napkins to the red wine which he was downing like a thirsty man. Hemingway was embracing his merriment and he giggled like he'd done in the very first refuge.

When things started to quieten down, I eventually picked up the courage to ask Hemingway about his daughter's death. He repeated what the Catalan had told us before moving on and telling us about his new son in India.

~

The Tale of How Hemingway Became a Father Again

After Manon's death, Hemingway struggled with the day-to-day. His work suffered and he and his wife divorced. Five years passed by, and a fifty-something Alsatian was on his way to India. This was not a random trip but he was going to meet a Tibetan orphan called Tenpa.

Hemingway's biological sons were all grown-up. He felt that he could do something for one of these orphans which he had heard so much about on television. Tibet had always been on his heart. It is a spiritual home for a lot of climbers. I have always envied the seven years Heinrich Harrer spent there when he and Peter Aufschnaiter escaped from a British camp in India (See: *Seven Years in Tibet*). I would have liked the opportunity to befriend the fourteenth Dalai Lama. Then there was China of course and now there are approximately 150,000 Tibetans living in exile. They are a long, long way from their uplands and they look forward to a time when the lamas will be their princes again. Many have fought and died for a free Tibet, and Hemingway felt that by adopting one of the orphans he too was helping in a little way.

Hemingway paid for Tenpa's education, food, clothing, and for his care whilst still being part of the exiled Tibetan community. The father would write to his son and his son would send him pictures of birds that flew above the compound in India. He'd press flowers and send them in abundance to his new father. Hemingway kept everything on a table in his bedroom. He had some pictures on his mobile. After about fifteen minutes, he found the right one. I was expecting a little boy but Tenpa was well into his late twenties by now.

As Hemingway talked, I imagined meeting Tenpa one day. Was he one of the famous *lung-pa* (wind men) who could speed like spirits across great distances? Colin Thubron's book was still fresh in my mind. I visualised Tenpa returning to Tibet and setting his eyes upon the scene that adorns Thubron's front cover: the egg-like mountain rising majestically from the yellow plain. Kailas. It looks like Nirvana. There's nothing on it; there is an emptiness which forbids even the *lung-pa* to float above its snow. Even the angels would be exposed on its harsh peak and would need crampons when their wings failed.

I continued my reverie as Hemingway spoke. I wondered whether Tenpa could levitate. I then heard Hemingway say Kath-man-du. (For some reason, the story had shifted to Nepal. I always mixed the two countries up anyway). I remembered how as a child I had thought that Kathmandu was full of cat-like men who crawled up the hillsides without rope or harness. Perhaps the real stories were different after all. I mean the stories of when the Western climbers reached the famous peaks for the so-called 'first' time. There they are with their oxygen tanks. Can you see them struggling along? They dream of strawberries, cream, hot baths and green fields; there they are nibbling some Kendal Mint Cake. But the bit they don't tell you is that they were always beaten there by a host of orange monks who would wait for them on the peaks with big grins on their faces.

'You've got to be joking!' one of the Englishmen shouts. 'Sherpa… what's going on!'

The Sherpa is as confused as the climbers.

'They're mad!' one of the other Western climbers shouts,

'We're all mad here. I'm mad. You're mad!' one of the monks responds in perfect Eton English. The climbers look at one another in astonishment.

'How do you know we're mad?'

'You must be,' now another cat-like monk purrs, 'or you wouldn't have come all the way up here.'

'Enough of this nonsense!' the Western leader interrupts. 'Excuse me gentlemen,' he is direct, 'would you tell us please, which way we ought to go from here?' The monks look at one another.

'That depends a good deal on where you're going,'

'We don't care where, as long as we get off this blasted hill!'

'Then it doesn't matter which way you go!'

I laughed inside whilst Hemingway continued his real story about Tenpa.

When visiting India, Hemingway found freedom in the mountains. The Pyrenees were foothills compared to those Asian kings. The paths up there are never marked and your life is always in danger. It takes time to get used to breathing. Some can't handle it. However, in those highest places, Hemingway discovered a lost relationship. Tenpa loved climbing too, and he even adopted his benefactor's surname.

He finished by saying that he was given a second chance. If there was a God, He had been good to him and whether he would meet this God would depend on how they would get on for the next couple of years. He showed me another picture of Tenpa and he looked just like a Sherpa climbing *Chomolungma*. He was another Tenzing Norgay leading Hemingway closer and closer to *Beyul*, the Buddhist pure lands, so close in sound to our Beulah, the holy land between heaven and earth.

～

We all went up to the dormitory together, spending the rest of the evening making fun of everything, especially Hemingway's clothes. He really stank and he spent hours washing his underpants, socks and tee-shirts in the bathroom sink with a little tub of washing powder Sylvie had given him:

'Sylvie offered to do my washing for me!' he was serious and very impressed. 'Not many houses does that, not even hotels. This is a good house. It is a good house indeed!' he said as he nodded for about a minute.

'She was going to wash your clothes?' my father asked.

'Yes. But I refused… but now I wish I had accepted.' He laughed as he carried on scrubbing his filthy garb. 'I wonder if she would marry me?!' We all laughed.

He then took us through how seldom he actually washed his clothes. He'd been walking for over a week and he was wearing the same, unwashed, garments.

'You should get Merino wool,' I interrupted.

'What is this?'

'It is wool that doesn't stink even after a week!'

'This is miraculous. Is it true?' He looked over at my father who was, as ever, looking over the map. 'Yep, it's true. You don't need to wash it.'

'That is quite amazing. Could you write the name of the material? Do they do socks?'

That night, Hemingway spoke non-stop until 2.30 in the morning. I can never remember Dad laughing so much and I wish that I could have recorded it all, but I suppose some things are best remembered. You need the face to accompany a joke and you need the mountain air to elevate it to its original hilarity.

The evening and the morning were the fifth day.

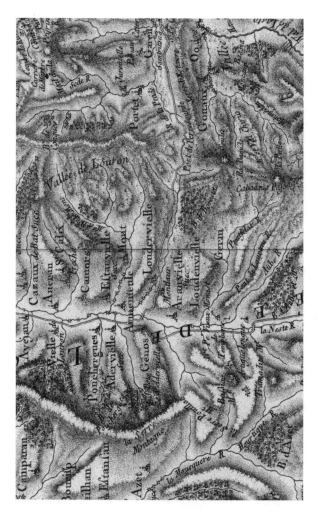

Map of the area around Banasque

6

Let us make now Man in our image, Man
In our similitude, and let them rule
Over the fish and fowl of sea and air,
Beast of the field, and over all the Earth,
And every creeping thing that creeps the ground.
This said, he formed thee, Adam, thee, O Man,
Dust of the ground, and in thy nostrils breathed
The breath of life; in his own image he
Created thee, in the image of God
Express; and thou becamest a living soul.

John Milton, Paradise Lost, Book VII

As I look for the chamois, I nearly bump into an adder
that is blocking my way. He looks at me now and I look
at him. He is completely still. A sudden bark frightens
him and he slithers in between two large white rocks.
The barking comes from a Patou (a Pyrenean sheepdog)
guarding the next field. The sun also rises higher now,
causing a shadow to emerge from my back. I am a
gnomon on a sundial, doubling in the light. How much
time have I spent up here?

The sixth day looked the easiest of them all. Our plan was to follow the GR10 over the Col de Val Louron-Azet (1580m), through the village of Germ, before picking up the car at Granges Estau. The room we were in reminded me of school camps: bunk beds, damp smell, flat pillows and cold nights. There was a picture of the Riviera on the wall. Perhaps this is where Sylvie really wanted to live before she married her husband. The sun was white hot and the warm oranges of the painting seemed to drip down to the floor. I could almost hear the cuckoo singing and the warm notes of Delius took me, for a moment, to some paradise garden. The smell of our breakfast ascended the steps. I walked over to Hemingway's bed. He was lying on his back with all his clothes on. He reminded me of a Breton *conteur* (bard) running through his store of stories for the evening. I poked him between his ribs. He mumbled. One of his eyes opened, the other one was firmly shut. I asked him whether he would be leaving La Bergerie that day:

'No, I will stay… At my age, if you find a good house you have to make the most of it,' he said as he closed his eye, 'after last night's meal, I would be crazy man to leave here so soon! My journey is only halfway whilst yours is nearly over.'

After about five minutes he got up and gravitated towards the stairs. Dad was already down there scoffing some ham and sheep's cheese. The tables looked naked

181

without the people that had adorned them the previous night. The black and white photographs of ancestors watched as my father ate his breakfast.

'Morning,' he said with his mouth full.

'*Bonjour,*' we both replied. Hemingway poured the coffee. Its aroma was pleasing. As he followed the breakfast ritual Hemingway was getting more and more emotional. He stopped spreading honey and held his knife aloft in his usual, grand manner.

'*Mes amis*, I will come and visit Wales and maybe stay with your family. We keep in touch. Please.'

'Of course,' Dad said.

'I feel that we are kin. The mountain has brought us to this place. To Azet of donkey and sheep fame. I will remember this great house. And I will remember you two as well.'

With this, he got onto his feet and waved his piece of bread around. A drop of honey landed on my arm as he did so.

'I will not forget you,' he stopped before starting again, 'as your singer Cheryl Bassey sing, we meet again, don't know when and they don't know where.'

'We'll send you an email.'

'And photographs if you please.'

'And photographs,' my father shook his hand.

He offered us some cigarettes and I, although tempted, thought about my nice, clean lungs, and refused politely.

We were sorry to leave behind both La Bergerie and Hemingway. The village was quiet. Hush, the animals were sleeping, the shepherds, the farmers, the grandmothers, the tradesmen and pensioners, schoolteacher, priest, drunkard, cheesemaker, the husband of the innkeeper and the children. The faithful four of the bus stop dreamt about Rhiannon whilst the mountains grazed on high air, drifting in and out of consciousness. They had seen so much, and yet, not much either. We passed by the graveyard. The spirits of yesterday were napping whilst guardian statues kept their eyes shut for a longer sleep than usual. Some of the graves had little photographs on them. Resistance fighters slumbered under the mountain soil and the curious mole was digging a new tunnel towards the road. He had seen a lot in his time too; Roman gold, rabbit holes, bones, more bones, crypts and underground passages. But the mole is blind so he would have bypassed all that and searched out the warm roots of ancient trees where his ancestors dug in past times. I went into the church. No sheep in there. The big shell font, the wooden pews and the face of the God-man re-imagined as a *berger* dying for his flock. The smooth grooves of the stones attest to the myriads that have passed the threshold and stared up at the berger king like that gathering on a Judean hill thousands of years ago.

The mountain views were majestic. The gaps in

the high cliffs were whitened with snow and the peaks looked like newly completed pyramids. They were topped with little spots which might have been climbers but were more likely to be summit stones. The clouds formed other sierras, rising and rising, until you realised that only your imagination could made mountains out of *cumuli*. The morning bells sounded from the campanile when the faithful four emerged and slowly walked towards the stop. Their daily shift had begun.

We left the borders of the village. The last house woke up with a cry which was probably the baby inside. I think that is where the shepherd family that we'd seen the night before lived. The grass was dew-grazed and before we knew it, a mist descended over us. It was as if some enchantment was robbing us of our views. This is a mist we know too well. I began to doubt whether I had actually seen the views in the first place because the clouds had blanketed everything in a grey and uncertain shade. I thought about the thick, Welsh, criss-cross blanket I used to hide under as a child. That was a warm comfort compared to this white and cold sheet. The droplets gathered in our hair, and our eyelashes were wet with the rest of the hill. The temperature dropped and we lost our sense of direction as the cairns and the angel's paint disappeared. In Celtic folklore, mist has always been an important motif. The Druid's Fog gave those ancients the ability to wrap themselves incognito and pass by their enemies undetected. The same spells were used for shape-shifting. Gwrhyr could change into a bird if he wanted to and St Patrick changed into a deer once. The Druid's Fog is different to Fairy Mist which appears without any warning. According to legend, the Fairy Mist was an omen of impending death. To me, the gloomy fog or the druidic mist is a condition that can seep into our minds. I had seen too many blue days and the sun of my childhood was still hot and bright – the mist was awful compared to these things. Above our heads, the summits flashed into view, giving us hope of deliverance from this heavy atmosphere.

~

Mount Carmel

'It was completely cloudless that day,' a father tells his son as they walk up the slopes of Mount Carmel. Olive and laurel trees guard the slopes whilst the sun breaks through near the highest point.

'Where are we going, Dad?' They walk together from tree to tree, making the most of the cooling shadows under the branches.

'God's vineyard.'

'God has a vineyard?'

'Yes and you will be his guest today. He has allowed

you to walk through his land.'

The father winks at his young son.

'That's good,' the boy pauses before leaping into the next question, 'what's on top?'

'Well, this mountain has seen a lot of things.'

'What things?'

'In the old days, the Pharaoh owned this land. He called it his holy headland. But there has been an altar to God here for a long time.'

'What's an altar?'

'It's where we give God things back. We thank him; we offer sacrifices; we communicate with him.'

The child struggles to keep up with his father. He grabs his coat. His little hand can barely hold on.

'What else?'

'What else what?'

'What else is on top?'

'Well, when I was your age, I saw Elijah on this hill.'

'Who's Elijah?'

'A Prophet or someone who speaks for God.'

'What was he doing up here?'

'God had taken the rain away. Your grandfather said that YAHWEH was angry because Ahab, the king, had turned our country to the false god, Baal.'

'A false god?'

'Yes a false god. One day, a tournament was announced between YAHWEH and Baal. All the Hittite priests gathered on the hill; hundreds of them, all adorned with golden earrings. Black painted lines were drawn under their eyes and their headpieces set them above the Israelites. So much noise. So much music. The king was over there. I can almost see him sitting there now in his chariot. The people followed these so-called priests up the hill. My father took me up to see as well.'

'What happened?'

'There was a hush and a wild-looking man came out of nowhere. His name was Elijah: a strong mountaineering prophet. The mountain was full of life and he was so full of life. The cliff edges seemed to move with all the people. But when he came, there was such a hush.'

They sit on some stones near the top. The father continues:

'You see those stones?'

'Yes'

'That's where it happened. He challenged the false prophets to call on their god and he would then call YAHWEH and the one who answered with fire was God. He also challenged the people to stop sitting on the fence, to decide whose side they were on. Some of the older ones started singing the songs of Israel but they were soon drowned out by the false prophets.'

'They shouted.

They sang.

They screamed.

They even cut themselves.

"'Baal! We cry to thee
Baal, Baal, Baal, Baal, We cry to thee, to thee, Baal
Baal, we cry to thee, cry to thee, Baal,
Oh Baal, our lord, we cry to thee
to thee we cry, Baal, Baal, Baal
holy Baal father of thunder, father of clouds, lord of
fertility, hear our prayer!'"

The boy could almost hear the false prophets as his father imitated their cries. He continued:

'The people knew that it was wrong but they watched and said nothing. Elijah screamed: "Is he sleeping? Is your god relieving himself in the bushes? Has the thunder god himself lost his bolts?" They cried all the louder and opened up the red streams in their arms and wrists.

"Baal! We cry to thee
Baal, Baal, Baal, Baal, We cry to thee, to thee, Baal
Baal, we cry to thee,
to thee, Baal,
Oh Baal, or lord, we cry to thee
to thee we cry, Baal, Baal, Baal
holy Baal father of
thunder, father of all the clouds, hear our prayer!"
It started to quieten down. Some died. The rest were exhausted.'

The father picks up a stick for his son. The hill seems to be breathing with the father's words. The little boy is completely quiet and he takes the stick from his father.

'Elijah stepped forward.'

The boy looks at his father and he imagines him to be Elijah. The father continues.

'I can see him now. He wore the skins of wild animals; his hair was mangled and dark; his eyes were flaming and he was frightening.'

The boy can almost see him.

'He told us all to come near… He stood at over six feet tall… and the people naturally stepped aside when he approached… He took some of the old stones up with tears in his eyes… I can remember thinking… there's nothing worse, and better… than seeing a strong man cry… But he did.'

The father touches some of the large stones that surround the cairn. He remembers how the prophet had ordered the people to pour water over everything to prove that if a fire came, then it would be no human fire.

'And when the strange job was done with all the water and the rocks, he lifted his arms up to heaven and prayed a quiet and heartfelt prayer.'

'What was it Pa, what did he say?'

'"Jehovah Elohim Abraham, Isaac and Israel, let it be known that you are Elohim in Israel and that I am your servant and I have done these things according to thy word." I can remember every word. The mountain woke up in anticipation as a great tongue of fire descended from heaven, licking the water up, and filling all the enemy with fear.'

'Fire?'

'Yes… It was God… The people cried out "Elohim is God; The Lord Jehovah, He is God!" I was terrified. I could see the prophet in the distance. My father took me away and I looked back as the prophet took up the sword. The mountain never forgot that day and neither have I.'

They walk towards the altar and the soil surrounding the stones is still stained by that supernatural fire.

Based on the events recorded in 1 Kings 18

~

Dad walked beside me. The click, click of our sticks hit the tarmac like the rhythm of a drum. The mist turned the sheep into spirits. From afar, they might have been those *kachina* dolls that the Native Americans used to make. I felt watched. Each hollow in the roadside cliff became an eye socket and the shadows in the rock humanised the edifices. I remember feeling like this in the Grand Canyon. Dad and I were walking on the North Kaibab Trail towards the Colorado River.

Before I knew it, the mountains lay down and formed canvases for my imagination.[19] I started thinking about the *Kachina*, those colourful spirits that lived in the creeks. I had seen pictures of masked *Kachina* dancers in *National Geographic*, four or five of them, orbiting campfires like celestial bodies. The dancers metamorphosed into their gods and I started seeing them in the night. I saw their controlled yet frantic movements develop into dynamo ecstasy charging the canyon with human energy. They were long gone but their *Kiva* was still there.[20] At night, the Pyrenean valleys turn into *Kiva*. All that was needed were for those sheep to become *Kachina* and to start splashing in the rivers and lakes before losing themselves in the starlight.

The mist continued to play tricks on us. We didn't know where we were going.

'Can you see any red and whites?' Dad asked.

'No. There are a few cairns but no red and white.'

We had wandered off the road and were trying to find our way across to the Col.

'This is not good, Nath…'

'It's a complete whiteout.'

'Ah, that may be one.' He spotted a faint red mark on one of the boulders.

We were fortunate. This was the right path and we

19 Kaibab – John Wesley Powell writes: 'This is called by the Indians "Kaibab" or "mountain lying down," so we adopted the name.'
20 Kiva – An underground temple where the Puebloans performed their rituals. The Kiva at Phantom Ranch Hostel dates from about 1050.

soon reached the main road again and the Col de Val Louron-Azet.

The Col de Val Louron-Azet has become famous for the part it sometimes plays in the Tour de France. The cyclists were here in 2013 for the Saint-Girons – Bagnères-de-Bigorre 168.5 km stage. Simon Clarke, an Australian, sprinted to the top of this col first before Ireland's Dan Martin took the stage at Bagnères. The roads are still scarred by colour. The tricolours of Ireland and France stand next to one another as a reminder of a common revolutionary past. The ghostly remnants of encouraging words are starting to fade as well but you can still make out the odd 'Go Froome!' which is repeated on every corner.

I remember going to see one of these cycling stages as a teenager. The road had been lined with the orange supporters of Euskaltel-Euskadi, a Basque cycling team well-known for its eager fans. The saffron racket only piped down if anything remotely Spanish was winning the race. After climbing to our spot, and eating some brebis and bread, a large carnival came through the village. It reminded me of Gabriel Garcia Márquez's Macondo in *One Hundred Years of Solitude* where the uproar of pipes and kettledrums announced the arrival of Melquiades and the gypsies laden with new and exciting inventions. Instead of magnets, astrolabes, compasses and sextants we were given freebies like hats, bottles, keyrings, babybels, bookmarks and, if you were really lucky, a cycling jersey. Some people might have sold their *burro* in order to get their hands on a cycling jersey. But I was a part of it too. I still have a spotty, King of the Mountains hat, which I acquired from one of the colourful floats.

The carnival had left a trail of solitude behind it, soon to be disturbed by the cyclists. Behind our spot, there was a small house where a French grandfather, in his armchair crow's nest, reported to his crew about the approaching cyclists thanks to the live coverage from TF1.

'Men ahoy!' (or something like that) he yelled from his Parker Knoll before causing a stampede of women, children and cats, all rushing to the pavement for a glimpse of Pierre Rolland, the village hero. The cyclists sped past. I can remember being amused at the grandfather in his chair. He didn't move an inch because his armchair proved better. I suppose he had seen the cyclists before and the motorbike cameras gave him a better view than the pavement ever could. The sea of colours and its spinning wheels was a grand end to the whole affair. It was very exciting and I am glad that I was able to see them all before the whole doping scandal scraped the colours away. The cyclists are still drawn to these hills though and their dreams are filled with red spots and a podium where they are crowned as mountain kings.

We descended the hill towards Loudenvielle. This

was an up-down, up-down day as we crossed all the valleys. The paths were occupied by mystified sheep who were wandering like clouds from the damp fields. As we walked up towards Germ we suddenly heard a deep and authoritative bark.

'Did you hear that?' Dad asked.

'A dog?'

'That's not a dog. That's a *Patou*.'

'Sounds like a dog to me.'

'It is a dog but it also *Patou*.'

There are two things which I fear in the mountains: thunderstorms and *Patou*. These mountain dogs initially look harmless enough. Their white fluffy coats have the same effect on people as Bambi, penguins, or a Koala bear would. The difference is that these dogs are dangerous and they are not called 'Great Pyrenees' for nothing. It's an old breed that bit and barked at the Gauls long before Belle and Sebastian came along. Marcus Terentius Varro describes the *Patou* in his *De re rustica* (On Agriculture) written thirty-seven years before Jesus was born:

> *In the first place, they should be procured of the proper age, as puppies and dogs over age are of no value for guarding either themselves or sheep, and sometimes fall a prey to wild beasts. They should be comely of face, of good size, with eyes either darkish or yellowish, symmetrical nostrils, lips blackish or reddish [...] large head, large and*

drooping ears [...] tail thick; with a deep bark, wide gape, preferably white in colour, so that they may the more readily be distinguished in the dark; and of a leonine appearance.

And the shepherds have used the *Patou* ever since. Varro repeats the word 'large' and they certainly can be. The puppies are placed with the lambs in the sheepfold. The Mowgli, sheep-cub dogs are then brought up thinking that they belong to the flock. For the first two years, the shepherd is careful not to pat or treat the dog like a pet – the dog has to bond closely with the sheep – and you do not pat sheep (especially when they're as ugly as Pyrenean ones). At least in Wales, the sheep look like sheep and their wool is thick and white. But a *Patou* defends his family till the end. When a wild animal or a strange shepherd approaches, the Patou gets up and springs into action. Before engaging, he barks very loudly. If the enemy does not retreat then *Patou* becomes a lion and fights if he needs to. These days, the shepherds are meant to erect signs as a warning, especially to walkers. Even if you see a sign, it's a whole different matter trying to locate the dog because their white bodies blend in with the sheep.

As we walked, we saw the source of the barking. His eyes were beady and his head was very large. We went the long way round but he continued to bark until we were well out of sight.

'He's good at blending in.' Dad held his stick like a sword. He took his rucksack and slipped his left arm through the straps like a shield.

'Great! I hate farm dogs.'

'Just be quiet!'

I took my rucksack off and got my ice-axe. I felt like doing a Gimli and saying, 'You have my axe, father!' We must have looked quite funny going round the field like Anglo-Saxon warriors. We didn't care. These Pyrenean dogs are more like the old-fashioned ones that we used to have in Britain. I imagine Gelert as some kind of *Patou*. Llywelyn Fawr left his prize hound to guard his baby's cot, knowing that Gelert would do his duty. One evening, a wolf broke in and darted at the child before Gelert intervened and ripped the wolf's throat with his sharp teeth. The wolf died, the child cried, and the bloody jowl of Gelert howled for his master. Llywelyn burst through the door and jumped to conclusions because he couldn't see the dead wolf or the living baby. His body reacted and his sword did its work swiftly and effectively. Then the baby cried. The Prince saw the wolf and his heart was broken when he realised that Gelert had probably saved his son's life. It's a good story. Not many modern breeds could kill a wolf but I reckon that the three-legged dog in the van together with the *Patou* would give it their best shot.

The dog's head moved and its eyes followed us until we were off his territory. He barked. Then again.

And again, until he was confident that my father and I weren't going to steal his sheep.

Recently, my father and I were walking in the Alps. We were somewhere between the town of Vallouise and a large ski resort high in the hills when darkness descended. We needed to find somewhere to sleep. It is difficult bivouacking on the hillside. We couldn't find anywhere flat enough without risking our bags rolling down the hill. We had a fading head torch and the hill was only illuminated by a single quad-bike light somewhere in the valley. Its bright light confused me. It was hard working out where the horizon was, where the sky started, and where the mountain finished. It was disorientating. The lights in the valley almost mirrored the stars, and I was happy when we finally found a ledge which would suffice. I had to dig a small boulder out of my space with my bare hands and then commit the optician's unthinkable sin and remove my contact lenses in the dark with dirty hands. We then lay down and enjoyed the stars (as much as I could without my contact lenses). Night progressed and the odd field mouse tickled my cheek. Dad had a migraine. Suddenly, there was a bark in the valley. Then another. And another. Bark after bark. I sat up. Got my phone and started shining my torchlight around looking for the pack of wolves that were producing this racket. Once again, there was a bark. And another. Bark, Bark,

Bark. As I listened, I realised that the first bark was the loudest. Dad stirred: 'It's one dog.'

'What do you mean?'

'The other barks are echoes. He's frightened by his own bark and he keeps barking at his own echo.'

That was such a comfort. The dog was much more frightened than we were. In my mind, that valley will always be 'Echo Valley' – a place where even the *Patou* are disorientated.

With the memory of the dog behind us, we finally arrived at another village. The rain returned and we were very wet again.

~

The Mount of the Magi

'Come up here. Look!' A man in a burgundy tunic is star-gazing from his chariot. His servant calms the horses down as the dust cloud reveals further chariots approaching. The Magi of Babylon have had to ride a long way from the city in order for the sky to be clear from all the light pollution. One of the older men had spotted a strange star from his observatory in the city and called for all the Magi to gather on the mountain. Not many answered his call.

'Where? Show me!' Another charioteer takes the

telescope-like instrument from the older man. 'You're right, it's moving.' The servants start recording on their clay tablets.

'Are you sure, Melchior?' another asks.

'Hassan, look!' The servants spot three camel riders and two horsemen.

'Salam,' the older man greets the other. 'Come and see!'

'Salam.' The Magi look upwards and are moved by the phenomenon. Their eyes speak a thousand words.

'Is there any other explanation?'

'It has to be what Belteshazzar spoke about.'[21]

'So long ago though… could it really be the sign of the Son of Man? A "star shall come out of Jacob?"'

The men are excited and their servants are instructed to ride back to Babylon:

'Quick. Shadrach and Hassan, go and prepare the caravan,' the older man turns to the others: 'I see him, but not now; I behold him, but not near; a star shall come out of Jacob…' they finish the verse together:

'…and a sceptre shall rise out of Israel!'

They ride back to the city because their journey has only just begun.

Based on events before the account in Matthew 2
with a reference to the prophecies in
Numbers 24: 15-17 and Daniel 9

~

21 Belteshazzar - the Babylonian name for Daniel.

Germ is a clean village. Hanging baskets and neat gardens adorn the houses well-built from skiing profits. In the centre of the village there is a fountain which used to be available for the *burros* and horses – an old-time fuelling station, I suppose. It has a long trough covered by a pagoda roof that doubles up as a shelter during heavy rain. We sat there for a break. I adjusted my poncho and Dad filled up the water bottles.

'Have you been here before?'

'No, I don't think so. Strange little place isn't it?' Dad looked around. 'Not a soul!'

The rain has a habit of emptying these villages, and the welcome you expect when you reach civilisation tends to consist of no more than a solitary, spooked-out cat. We walked through the village like intruders into an empty house. The doors creaked and the homes were not very homely. A long building, like some kind of Viking Hall, marked the end of the village. We rang the doorbell. No answer. I tried the door and it opened with a clattering of beads.

'Hello there!' Dad called through the hall.

'Is there anyone here?'

'Hello!' Dad started wandering about.

A large chef came out of the kitchen.

'We have no room, I'm afraid. Many schoolchildren staying here.'

'Really?'

'Yes hundreds… They are hiking as we speak.'

I don't know whether he was lying or whether he just didn't want any guests that night.

'Very well,' Dad interrupted the awkwardness, 'may we trouble you for some coffee?'

'Of course… I will have to microwave it though.'

'I'm sorry?' Dad's face looked absolutely puzzled as he struggles to hide some expressions.

'I only have drip coffee. I'm afraid it has gone cold. But it's fine to microwave. I'll knock fifty cents off the price.'

'Many thanks. Very kind of you.' Dad was being sarcastic.

We sat on two chairs listening to the sound of a microwave for two long minutes. I looked at Dad and he looked at me and the fat man was sweating even though it was really cold in the building. He was very strange. The ping deserved a hallelujah.

'Milk?' he asked.

'Black!' we answered in unison. After burning our lips, we paid a euro for probably the worst coffee in Christendom and left as soon as we could. It was that kind of coffee that lingered for a long time in your mouth.

'That must have been days old,' Dad said as we walked on the wet road with the rain accompanying us like background music.

'You think?' I looked at him. He made a face.

'Worst coffee I've ever had and it's wet.'

'I've had worse.'

'Really?'

'Oh yes. I had chicory coffee once. That was bad.'

'Never had that.'

'I don't recommend it.'

We took the GR10 for a bit longer before joining the D618, north of all the ski hotels. The D618 is the road that goes over another famous col, the Col de Peyresourde (1569m). Since 1910, the Tour de France has crossed this col many times. The valley is long and green and at the end you can see a little gap of sky which takes you down towards Luchon, the old spa town.

We thumbed a lift again and this time a really deaf man welcomed us into his car. He shouted every sentence and his English was poor.

'*Bonjour*! ENGLISH! GET IN! VERY WET YES? LUCHON? YES? COME IN!'

Dad thanked him and finally got to do that thing which Englishmen love doing: shouting at a foreigner as if they're deaf. This time the guy really was deaf. I laughed to myself.

'THAN-nk yOOOu VEER-y much Monsieur. LUCHON please. Thanks, I mean, MERCY-I.'

Before long, conversation entered that realm where everyone starts grinning before slowly turning one's head towards the window. However, the view wasn't that great. He drove through the col in the wrong gear, and I saw a gathering of cyclists watching us before taking selfies against the rainy vista. For some of them, it was a #LifeGoal cycling up the Peyresourde – pity about the weather.

The driver dropped us off at the turn-off for the village of Oô which meant that we had come full circle. The rain made it a bit of an anti-climax. Dad got a lift with a shepherd to get the car at Granges Estau so I sat in a bus stop like those guys in Azet. Instead of a pretty girl, a dog ran past me like he was escaping for his life. This happened four times: backwards and forwards, backwards and forwards. I don't think he liked the rain and I found it hilarious. Eventually he wore himself out and he was nearly knocked over by my father's Skoda Yeti. We left the poor dog in the rain and we drove down the valley to Luchon.

But the trip was not over yet. Dad was determined to climb a couple more peaks before the end. We booked into the Hotel de Paris and ate that night with all the old people who looked like they'd holidayed in this place since the beginning of time. This was one of those spa hotels where all the meals are the same, the hospital is next door, and the baths are just thirty yards away. The smell of sulphur seeps through the windows and the ghosts of 'water-takers' stroll down the boulevards in top hats and parasols. I slept well that night and dreamt of home again.

~

The Tale of Hemingway and Myrddin

I was back in Carmarthenshire, wandering the wooded hills near Pantllyn. The lake was just below me and the limestone caves twisted and turned somewhere underneath me. I felt like a mole on the surface. Out of place.

On the road, there is a curious signpost. It looks like your usual road sign with its red border and white background. The difference with this sign is that it has a big picture of a toad on it. On autumn nights, around eight hundred toads cross the road and ascend to their winter quarters on the hill. They pass the swinging tyre and go somewhere. In my dream, I could see the froggy host coming up from the lake. It is a magical lake because it is the only turlough in Wales (there are many in Ireland). Every year, the water completely disappears from the lake and it fills up again later on. It's basically a giant bath with a lot of frogs in it.

I ascended my childhood hill, and remembered stumbling across an old lime kiln where my friend and I were startled by a bat. I passed it and the shadows of yesterday appeared. I carried on and entered a cave. It was so dark. I went deeper and deeper before coming across a collection of huge bones huddled in the corner. They were giants' skeletons. I ran out of the cave.

That's when I saw the curious figure again. I mean, the man on the white stag. I ran like a beast and managed to keep up with him. He entered the black forest and dodged the mountain-ash trees. The leaves fell as we passed and they sometimes stayed on my body as if I was familiar to them. I chased him and tried to work out his identity in my sleep. He could have been *silvester homo* who was known to spend his time gazing on the wild beasts grazing in the glades. He eats the fruit of herbs; he eats herbs; he eats the fruit of the trees and the berries of the bramble bush. He is like a wild animal, sleeping outside, and staring at the stars from the high peaks.

I was getting closer. I could almost touch him. He was wearing a grey cloak.

We reached the top of the quarry. The whole of Carmarthenshire seemed to spread itself beneath us and we passed my hinterland: the den, the battlefields, the place we shot a hundred enemies, the place where we built a dam and basked in the water with glory before jumping out because a leech had attached itself to my leg, the place where we found a fossil, the place where we spied on druggies, the place where we found chicken bones, the place where we found a pentagram drawn in chalk across the road which my little sister hurriedly brushed away with her foot, the place where we tried to save a dying woodpigeon, the place where we ate the wrong berries and got sick, the place where my sister fell into a dark water hole, the place where the stallion chased my sister, the place where we met a fierce dog, the place where the farmer stole our treehouse timber, the place where my deaf next-door neighbour and I fought a duel with catapults and crab apples, the place where we found a footprint and invented stories about its owner, the place where the old bottles were thrown, the place where I preached to the trees, the place where we discovered hundreds of tiny black spiders, the place where we gathered conkers, the place where the old plough was rusting away, the place where the old ruined cottage was sinking into the ground, the place where the rhododendron plant had got out of control, the place with the little hidden bridge, and the place where darkness finally drove us home.

I was getting closer and closer. But I couldn't quite stop him.

The figure sped along the top like a man drunk on air. The quarried landscape appeared before me. I recognised Llandybie in the distance and the lights of Carmel, Pantllyn, and Milo breaking up the darkness with orange streaks. I could just make out my old primary school – I cursed it and was glad that its miserable four walls no longer imprisoned me. Horses grazed in its yard and the windows were broken by stones and neglect. I looked forward to the day that its bricks are taken away, one by one. Suddenly, a light flickered in the distance and the fox, which lived in my garden, gave a loud bark.

I came across a bench with two figures sitting there hand in hand. They looked like lovers. They turned to us suddenly. The man had a moustache and there was fear in his eyes. He seemed familiar. The hooded figure stopped. He took his hood off.

There was an awkward silence. I half expected the fat man to appear with chicory coffee out of the woods or one of those blonde witches or mushroom gatherers. But no. The rider made a sudden movement. He tore one of the antlers from the stag. The woman screamed as he stretched back and hurled the antler in the air. I could hear it flying like a boomerang
                              until it
                      penetrated
                  the throat
            of the
      man on the bench.
I looked at the stag
      and was glad,
            that a new antler
                  had already grown in
                        the wound's place.

I eavesdropped, and worked out that the woman's

name was Guendoloena, the unfaithful wife of the hooded man, Myrddin.

~

The evening and the morning were the sixth day.

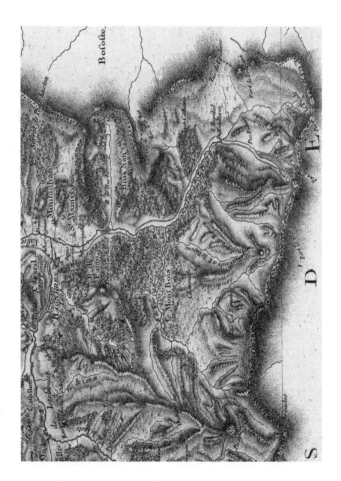

Map of the area around Banasque

7

Thus the heavens and the earth were finished, and all the host of them. And on the seventh day God ended his work which he had made; and he rested on the seventh day...

Genesis

At the end of the beginning, God rested in the Pyrenees. He could have gone on but having seen this good and unspoilt work, he was overwhelmed.

6 a.m. Old people could hear the birds' matins even though most of them are deaf. As we approached the dining room, we weren't surprised to see a number of chino-clad ancients accompanying us to the watering hole. If you listen to these mundane moments, they are as polyphonic as the Serengeti; the sound of shuffling trousers, the newspaper rattle, the uncontrolled coughing and the tinkle of an old woman's curiosity as she investigates every container on the buffet table with the dedication of a crime-scene analyst.

Bagnères-de-Luchon (commonly referred to as Luchon) is a place where white heads are tinged with the memory of colour. The forty-eight thermal springs are impregnated with sodium sulphate, making it sound old in itself. The Allées d'Étigny acts like the backbone of the town. The long road lined with bars, shops, and parked cars, fleshes out in a stream of lime trees which splashes the pale stones with a green hue completing the spectacular Pyrenean backdrop. Antoine d'Étigny (1719-1767) was an important man here. The steward of Auch not only tried to introduce Merino sheep (Hemingway might even be wearing those socks by now) but he also re-vivified the thermal baths which had been obsolete since Roman times. He is just a statue now – white and Marley-like – guarding his baths at the southern extremity of the allées. The merry-go-round is covered and the old Napoleon III era casino declares a past that cannot return. The passers-by perambulate along the ghostly boulevards like shadows. One ancient could still make a lot of noise; his name is Abraham and he is a bronze bell born in 1596. I can't remember hearing him, though.

It was our last day in the Pyrenees and we would be finishing our trip with a border crossing near Hospice de France. We drove to a car park just below the hospice as the taste of instant coffee dried up my mouth. Pylons had replaced angels and the streams were filled with concrete as EDF did its damming work. But as we got higher we neared the earth again. The old meeting places were being re-established and we knew that the pylons would soon disappear. I saw a big pig sleeping in a field.

'Has Mamgu ever told you about her father?' I asked Dad as I saw the pig. (No, don't worry reader; the pig didn't fall on him from the trees).

'What do you mean?'

'Seeing that pig reminded me of it.'

'Why?'

'Her father – when everything got too much – would wander down to the pig sty and smoke some cigarettes, open a bag of Fox's Glacier Mints, and read Matthew Henry's *Bible Commentaries* on a milking stool. She told me that her father looked like that guy in the *Up* movie with the balloons.'

Hospice de France is another place where *burros* live. There's about three of them there, clip-clopping around the buildings, feeding on climbers' sandwiches and suffering from the harsh treatment of the guardian who shoos them away from any friendly encounter. The hospital/hospice does not have doctors. Before the current buildings, the Knights Hospitaller (Knights of Malta) built a station here around 1200 A.D. in order to control and monitor the passage of the Port de Venasque (or Banasque) – a border-crossing 2444m above sea level. The Knights set up headquarters at Frontés (see top of map between Montauban and Juzet-de-Luchon) and established stations at key points along the border. Their simple goal was to control these passages through the mountains, especially when the road between Luchon and Banasque became a secondary route on the Camino de Santiago. These stations provided the pilgrims and merchants with protection as well as a place of refuge in bad weather. Eventually the Order abandoned the region when the people (guided by the priests) realised the economic benefits of holding such a position in the mountains. But the knights are still here because the donkeys still wear prominent crosses on their backs.

In the 1830s, the Scottish adventurer, James Erskine Murray came on a similar trek. His book, *A Summer in the Pyrénées* (1837), describes the moment he arrives at the Hospice:

> *A two hours' ride along the banks of the Pique brought us to the Hospital of Luchon. This building is what in Scotland would be called a shealing, one half of which is devoted to the accommodation of travellers, the other used as the permanent residence of a strong party of douaniers, who are stationed here to prevent smuggling upon a district of the frontier upon which it is next to impossible to do so effectively.*

One half is now a hostel/café and the other has been made into a museum. This area has always been full of soldiers. From the white-crossed uniforms of the Maltese order to the Nazis who gunned down a group of Resistance fighters nearby. The Port was used as an escape route and its strategic position means that they even had a checkpoint built during the 'War of the Pyrenees' (1793-1795) – the soldiers must have been freezing up there.

We passed the donkeys and saw a big, stone dragon tooth stuck in the ground. My mother and father came to this place when they were first married. Dad knew what the stone was.

'It's a memorial for escapees during the war,' he said as I noticed the Lorraine Cross carved into the stone. This old Christian cross was meant to be an answer to the twisted swastika. Spilled blood dyed the immaculate river and bullets sped in the vibrant woods as I imagined men and women crouching in the undergrowth, waiting for the right moment to escape.

'Let's go,' Dad said, as he adjusted his bag and carried his burden up the hill. Each tree became a station on this *via crucis*. How many sacrifices were offered in this place? In the middle of the forest, trees disappeared again until only a couple remained.

~

The Two Hills

'I have never seen anything like this, sir,' a Roman soldier is talking to the *centurio supplicio præpositu*.[22]

22 According to Roman custom the centurion who presided over execution.

'I know. When did it start?'

'From the sixth hour.'

'I see.'

Golgotha is a dark hill. In Aramaic, it means the place of the skull. A group of soldiers are stationed whilst any execution takes place. Their commanding officer has just arrived on the scene. A strange darkness, like an eclipse, has covered the area.

'What's that noise?' They hear screams.

'I don't know. It's getting darker sir.' The soldier answers.

As he says these words the earth begins to shake.

'What was that!'

'Hold your ground! Men... create a perimeter.' The centurion blows his whistle and the guards pick up their weapons. The ground around Golgotha seems to be breaking. It is quiet again.

'They say he is a king,' the second in command says to the centurion.

'Who?'

'The third man, sir. The one in the middle.' There is a lot of shouting in the distance and a young boy runs up to the officer: 'Speak. Quickly!'

'Sir, there is report of people being raised from the dead.' They all look at one another. Behind the crosses, one of yesterday's executions seems to be stirring.

'Hold your ground, men!' He speaks to himself: 'What manner of man was this?'

The boy runs away and the centurion looks at the third figure on the cross. The soldier next to him coughs whilst the crowds disperse in fear.

The bowed figure is dead. He is naked and torn. The crown he wears is thorny and his feet are like crampons clinging on to a steep wooden slope. The soldier looks at him for a while and tries to understand. This is very difficult for him.

'Truly this was *theou huios* (Son of God).'

Eventually he leaves the spot and bumps into two Jews on his way back. Their eyes are wet. One of them looks like a Rabbi.

Some days later, the centurion receives a report from one of his men.

'Sir, they say his followers have stolen the body. The Sanhedrin is furious.'

'He is risen?'

'Sir?'

'Is he risen?' He stands up.

'There is no body, sir. Some say that he has been spotted walking towards a mountain.'

The centurion takes his most sturdy hobnailed sandals and straps them firmly around his feet and ankles. He takes his staff and hurries out of the room, leaving the soldier without even saying goodbye.

Based on the account documented in Matthew 27

~

The valley was getting higher and higher until it suddenly filled with cloud. The plan was to reach the Refuge de Venasque (2239m) before heading up to the port itself where we would take a right-hand turn towards the Pic de Sauvegarde (2738m), the first Pyrenean peak my father ever climbed. The path was clearly marked and we developed a steady pace for a couple of hours.

Whilst having a quick drink, we saw a troop of very fit-looking French walkers catching us up from behind. For some reason, we had to beat them and the race was on. My father started cutting through the snake bends, taking a more direct route up the hill, but this was tiring. Nevertheless, I followed him, determined not to let the French beat us to the col. A man in a baseball cap was their pacemaker; he was quick and determined. But that is where they made a fatal mistake. He was going so quickly that the chap in the back was starting to struggle; he fell behind before eventually begging the others to slow down.

'Dad, they've stopped!' I was watching them closely. We were directly above them but still quite a way ahead.

'Okay. Quick! We can make some ground here.' We metamorphosed into schoolboys because it became a battle. 'They've started again!' I pushed Dad along.

'We've got a bit of an advantage now... Don't stop… Stop looking back… keep going.' Dad was panting.

It was silly but fun. The col came into sight and a sign indicated that we were getting nearer to the refuge finishing line. The refuge looked like a bungalow with a big blue box attached to it; this was much smaller than the other refuges we had seen. The wiry aerials and the scientific equipment dotted around the valley took me forward a thousand years to a scene where men have set up camp on a different planet. A little weather station seemed to move by itself with its various turbines and laboratory sounds. As we approached the freshly-painted blue door, we realised that we had won and celebrated by sitting on a very cold bench in the cloud and I became excited by the prospect of a Fanta *Naranja.* We noticed a tent in the field nearest to the lake. The zip opened and a man in his sixties, wearing a white beard and a hippie bandana, strode out on a pair of wiry legs. It was as if he had been hibernating for a decade.

The Refuge de Venasque

'*Bonjour!*' he shouted, whistling a tune from one of Verdi's operas. I decided that this was a real marsh-wiggle straight from the pages of C.S. Lewis's Narnia.

'*Bonjour!*' We both answered.

'*Ca va?*'

'*Bon, bon*,' my father answered. 'Are you the guardian?'

'No, I am not. My son is the guardian. He is busy at the moment though. Can I help you?'

The marsh-wiggle brought us our Fanta and plonked the cold cans on the table. We could see him up close now; he had a young face.

'We're heading up to Pic de Sauvegarde,' Dad told him.

'Yes, very nice path and the weather looks good too.'

He pointed to a cloudy sky and we could see a little blue window open up near the Port. We downed the ambrosia, and as we finished, the four French climbers passed us without saying bonjour.

From the refuge, the path looked as if it were going straight into the rock. I couldn't see the door and I definitely couldn't believe that there was a crossing somewhere into Spain. It looked like a complete dead end. We sat down for a while.

'You sure there's a door, Dad?'

'Yes. Trust me. I can remember this place well.'

'But even the path seems to fizzle out,'

'I know but you'll see soon enough.'

Looking around I realised how quiet it was again. The Earth seemed so young. William Blake once said that great things are done when men and mountains meet. I say that greater things happen when somebody stays in the mountains for seven days or more. New worlds are formed, dreams merge with reality; those things which are impossible, or that you wouldn't dream of doing, become possible in these higher places. I looked at Dad and wondered how his seven days compared to mine. Maybe, like Moses, he had seen the burning bush and spied on angels conversing on the cols. I had no right to intrude. We sat there in silence as words became more and more unnecessary.

Col de L'Iseran (2270m). My first Col.

Some time went by. We were tired. The path was a good one and Dad suddenly said something out of the blue:

'I remember taking your mother up Cadair Idris… We hadn't been married very long and she thought it would be nice if she tried to come along, you know.'

'What happened?

'To begin with, she somehow got stuck on some scree and then she had an asthma attack!' We laughed.

'Has she been up anything else?'

'Not really. I think that took the wind out of her.'

But Dad exaggerates all the time. The truth is that I have seen a lot of photographs where both Dad and

Mam are up some hill somewhere. (But Mam's Cadair Idris experience wouldn't be that funny then). One of my favourite photographs is the one which, I think of as my real genesis mountain. Mam is taking the picture. She is probably wrapped up in scarves and a big hat. The cold air would definitely have given her bad asthma. Dad is looking at her nose and maybe an eye which is allowing her to spy through the lens of her giant Olympus camera. My father is standing near the Italian border in his red raincoat. The hills behind him are cotton wool white, and in his coat, I am sleeping. This Alpine baptism was my first mountain and both my parents were present.

~

The Mount of Transfiguration

They reach the peak of *Har Tavor* (Mount Tabor). James and John rest on some stones. Their staffs clatter on the rock as they let them fall. Peter looks out towards Jezreel and surveys the different movements below. He remembers the stories about Deborah the prophetess and how Sisera was defeated nearby. He longs for the days that Israel would be free. He looks over at their guide. Yeshua touches the cairn and looks at Peter. They pray together.

Some time passes, and a cloud moves over the hill. The three disciples are sleepy and Yeshua gets up and walks around the peak. Peter wakes up: 'John, look!'

'What?'

'Look at Yeshua.'

Their guide's face is brighter than the sun and his raiment turns white. They cover their faces because they're terrified. He stands in glory and the mountain becomes holy.

'Who are they?' James whispers.

Two figures come and stand beside Yeshua. One looks like John the Baptist. His face is weathered but, in some strange way, it's been re-made. His hands look hard but yet they're soft. The other man has a long beard but he looks young. Both men bow at the foot of Yeshua. The three disciples know who they are. It is Moses and Elijah – the two mountaineering prophets.

A voice comes from above saying: 'This is my beloved Son, in whom I am well pleased; hear ye him.' The voice frightens them. The light is bright and they feel as if the mountain is about to open up and swallow them. They fall flat on their faces and weep like children.

And Yeshua comes and touches them, saying, 'Arise, don't be afraid.' They look up and Yeshua is leaning on his staff. He is a climber again.

Based on the accounts recorded in Matthew 17, Mark 9,

Luke 9, and mentioned by one of the eyewitnesses in 2
Peter 1: 16-18

~

We walked further and further away from the Refuge de Venasque and suddenly, the doorway came into view. Murray describes the same place:

Another staircase, similar to the last, but, if possible, still steeper, and rendered slippery by the melting snow, is ascended before arriving at the base of the high ridge of rock in which is the Port of Venasque. The Port is formed by a narrow slit in this wall of rock, so narrow and confined, that it almost would have been possible to have supposed it the work of man if a glance at the immense height of the rocks through which it leads did not convince us that nature alone had opened up this passage.

I looked at the doorway. The sky seemed to penetrate the rock. The arrowhead testified to the warring forces of down here and up there. There is another place in the Pyrenees called La Brèche de Roland where a gap was created in the mountain after Count Roland tried to destroy his great sword *Durendal* having lost the Battle of Roncesvalles in 778. The narrow slit at Venasque used to be narrower until it was enlarged for horses sometime in history.

The Port de Venasque (French side)

The Port is charged with stories. The rock itself seems to be straining with the voices that have been heard passing from one side to the other. Dad told me how a large group of women and children apparently froze to death when escaping during the Spanish Civil War.

This was a gateway to freedom for so many but it was also a dark and deadly place. I thought about Machado again, especially when I saw the blue skies on the other side. I wondered when he actually wrote that line. Did he know that death was nearing? Had he glimpsed the other side? Life is a walk that walks you and eventually another path begins. I cannot believe that a journey simply stops. Each path leads somewhere or another path which begins where the last one finishes. I walked through the door in the rock and, as I did so, something odd happened. The weather changed suddenly, and a year later, I found out that Murray had also experienced exactly the same thing over a hundred and fifty years before:

The phenomenon was curious, and its interest greatly heightened, from the situation in which it took place. The mist, rolling up the valley through which we had passed, was, […] the moment it encircled the edges of the high ridges which separated the countries, thrown back, as it were, indignantly, by a counter current from the Spanish side. The conflicting currents of air, seemingly of equal strength, and unable to overcome each other, carried the mist perpendicularly from the summits of the ridge; and filling up the crevices and fissures in its uneven surface, formed a wall many thousand feet above it, of dark and (from the appearance of solidity which its massive and perpendicular character bestowed upon it) apparently impenetrable matter.

The Port (Spanish side)

The cloud seems to be alive. It took me back to the Sinai Peninsula when God appeared to the Israelites like a pillar of cloud. He led them by the day in this manner and at night-time he came as a pillar of fire. I half expected the clouds to catch alight but they didn't. The clouds were more like the Celtic mist which brought discomfort. As we walked through, the cloud formed a long finger which seemed to make a grab at Spain and at the same time try to get hold of Dad. France would not let us depart its cloudy valley and we felt pursued by the gloomy mist. Before us was the Maladeta, (3312m) or the cursed or damned mountain, which is very close to the highest peak, Aneto (3404m). I suddenly remembered the Catalans and for some strange reason I felt sick. At the time I didn't know why.

'I climbed those in my thirties,' my father said, 'I wouldn't do it again'.

'Why?'

'I needed a rope off the second one and two Germans helped me a lot. It was just unpleasant!'

Dad had told me stories about the time he climbed Aneto. I think it scared him. We rested near the doorway for a while and watched the somnambulant hills shifting up and down like pulsating bodies.

~

The Mount of Ascension

It was their last hike. Forty days had passed since the Resurrection.

Yeshua is walking with his friends. They return to Olivet and pass through the olive trees. Yeshua picks some olives and eats with them. His hands flash before them and the nail marks haunt them. But they are happy.

They reach the peak.

Peter, James and John half expect the whole host of heaven to descend. They've already met Elijah and

Moses. But Yeshua faces them.   Up
He drops his staff   Up
and a great cloud envelops him.   Up
Before they know it, he starts ascending. Up until a
cloud receives him out of sight.

'You men of Galilee!' The men look around and see
two walkers sitting on the cairn.

'Yes?' Peter answers on their behalf.

'Why are you standing there gazing up at heaven?'

The disciples look around and are amazed at the
manner of the pair. They realise that these mountaineers
are sent by YAHWEH.

'The same Jesus, which is taken up from you into
heaven, shall come in like manner as you saw him
going up in the clouds.' The two men disappear and the
disciples prepare for their day's descent to Jerusalem.

Most of these climbers would die in the years following
this descent. One would follow his guide to the cross
in Italy, where he was crucified upside down. One
went as far as Russia and was crucified on his way
back to the uplands of Greece. One was stabbed in
India. Another one went to the dunes of Africa and
was cruelly killed by a Roman. One supposedly died
in the hills of Ethiopia whilst preaching. One went to
Arabia and did not return. Others died in Syria, Persia,
and Jerusalem. Only one of the climbers survived and

lived to a good old age. They gave their lives, not to a mountain, but because they were eyewitnesses to the one who made the mountains.

Before he died, one of the climbers explained why they were willing to be put to death in a letter to his friends:

> *For we have not followed cunningly devised fables, when we made known unto you the power and coming of our Lord Jesus Christ, but were eyewitnesses of his majesty. For he received from God the Father honour and glory, when there came such a voice to him from the excellent glory, 'This is my beloved Son, in whom I am well pleased.' And this voice which came from heaven we heard, when we were with him in the holy mount.*

He was killed not long after writing these words. He never forgot his time in the hills.

Based on the gospel accounts and 2 Peter 1:17

~

The last mountain we climbed in the seven days was called Sauvegarde. As I said, this had been my father's first Pyrenean peak. It had its difficult sections. Scree, sharp rocks and slippery grass soon gave way to scrambling which led to a magnificent peak giving us a view over the cloud sea of France and the valley of Benasque on the other side. The hilltops looked like islands scattered in the sea – a Pyrenean archipelago. We ate some peanuts on the peak and realised that the Frenchmen had beaten us up there. They said bonjour and we were a little bit gutted but smiles were exchanged and Anglo-French amities continued.

We descended the mountain quickly and started heading towards the next col that would lead us back into France. In the valley, we met another Catalan man who had dreadlocked hair and a small dog peeping out of his rucksack. He greeted us:

'*Hola.*'

'*Hola,*' we answered, noticing that he looked a little low.

'Where you come from?' he asked, knowing that we weren't local. My father told him about our trip and how we had walked a circuit in and out of Spain before having this extra day from Hospice de France.

'Did you hear about those climbers on Aneto?'

'No, what happened?' Our Catalan friends at d'Espingo and Portillon came to my mind. I had heard about the young Scottish boy that had died with his father in the 90s and apparently seven people passed away near or on Aneto during the summer of the previous year. I felt sick.

'They were Catalan climbers,' he continued. It had obviously had an effect on him, 'I think a party went

up and two of them slipped on the glacier.'
He pulled out his phone and showed us the headline:

'*Dos muertos en el Pirineo se suman a un trágico
verano que casi duplica la cifra de 2014.*' [23]

From what I understood, this year had been worse
than the previous year, because thirteen in total had
died. One of the mountaineers was a fifty-two year old
from Gava near Barcelona.

'Apparently,' the guy continued, 'he slipped over 200
metres.'

I felt sicker, not knowing if these were the knights
that we had spent time with in the Refuges. Had their
quest been fatal? Had they fallen on the Bridge of
Muhammad, that short rocky passage that leads to the
summit? The ice must have vanished beneath him as
he ran. Did he see the peak, I wonder – a luminous
star – hanging there like an unreachable chalice? I do
not know to this day whether they were the same men
or whether the Catalan was talking about a different
party. Whoever they were, it shook me, and I thought
about the poor climbers' families at home.

We hiked up to the Port de la Picade (2529m),
feeling extremely thirsty. Failing to find any water, we
eventually crossed the Port, still depressed after hearing
about the dead climbers. On entering the cloud again,

23 Two dead in the Pyrenees contributes to a tragic summer, almost doubling
the fatalities of 2014.

we passed a group of four Australian students. One was causally urinating near the cairn and the others were sitting down, not knowing that there was a glorious view just 20 metres away from them. I heard them saying how miserable the day was – they would soon experience the blue skies which we had just walked out of. One of them wanted to turn back and I was so glad that they did not.

We followed the border for a while. The path went through a knife-edge ridge which opened up before us like a way carved through the stone. Rocky shelves acted like ramparts on each side and a smooth thoroughfare turned the mountain into something like the Great Wall of China. The cloud hid the valleys on both our left and right and I can't remember seeing anything except for a herd of goats, who interrupted our path. They came up to us and started licking our hands. It was very strange but I guess they liked the salt. I stopped for a moment. I looked ahead and my father kept appearing and disappearing, depending on the mood of the cloud.

The rocky walls soon dissolved in the mist and we were walking on a high green plateau. Now and again, a cairn would lead us forwards. I was walking for a while with a foot in each country. This was strange. I didn't know which I preferred and when the path started turning up again, I felt tricked by the cloud and by the goats and by my father.

I felt as if the clouds would take me to some other range where the climbers were equipped with hind's feet and where the air was light, and the water sweet. The Pevensie children climb those hills in the last Chronicle of Narnia. They end up in the high mountains. There is no snow on those mountains: there are forests and green slopes and flashing waterfalls, 'one above the other, going up for ever'.

Soon afterwards, the Great Lion comes 'leaping down the cliff like a living cataract of power and beauty'. It's one of my favourite bits of the Narnia stories. After that, they go further up and further in to the real England. Perhaps I was nearing the real Pyrenees.

I thought I had reached the top of the valley but the mountains carried on and on.

Some areas are still forbidden.

They are forbidden until the sun burns the clouds on its altar, which may give me access to those higher sierras.

Hemingway's Postscript

Hello!

It is a pleasure to read your message. My trek in the Pyrenees is achieved since the 30th of September. Now I am back to Mulhouse (Alsace) and I'm preparing my travel to India which starts the 19th November. I'm very glad of my 7 week trek through the mountains, it was a very good experience, indeed. I will not forget our meeting at Espingo and Azet. When I reached at Baysellance, the weather was very cold and stormy and when I left the next day the Vignemale was covered by snow... I enjoyed very much Ayous Refuge, which you recommended to me. I was lucky because the next day was the last before closing. Soize de Floch and her friends were very busy for cleaning and preparing the refuge for winter season. I spent also one night at Horquette d'Arrê which is a high pass and where I found one shelter which has just been repaired by a group of volunteers. It was also very cold there... I could see four bears (Myrtille with her children Diego, Segalene, and another one but I forget his name) at Borce – Parc 'Ours.

Thanks a lot for your invitation. My projects are fixed for one year, then after, everything is possible, including Wales or Scotland.

My very best greetings to you and the family,
We keep in touch,
Friendly yours,
> *'Hemingway'*

Acknowledgements

I am so grateful to all the storytellers who made this book possible. *Diolch yn fawr*.

Thank you to Parthian books for their continual support. Many thanks to Richard Davies, Susie Wild, Robert Harries and Alison Evans for your hard work. I am also very grateful to Gwen Davies for her meticulous editorial work and for her encouragement throughout the project. An earlier edition of this work came second in the New Welsh Writing Awards 2016 which was judged by Gwen and by Rory MacLean. I am grateful to both. I am also very thankful to the Welsh Books Council for financially supporting the publication.

I would also like to thank the David Rumsey Map Collection and the University of Bern for giving me permission to use the various maps.

I also owe a huge debt to my friends and colleagues. I am extremely grateful to Katie Gramich, my PhD supervisor who has supported me (and has been patient with me) for many years as both a supervisor and a friend. I am also grateful to all my friends and colleagues in Cardiff who have sat through long conversations about hills, religion and everything else under the sun. I am especially indebted to Carwyn Shires and Katie Lewis, who read and commented on early sections of *Seven Days*.

Merci beaucoup Patrice Bechler and all the other mountain friends we met along the way.

I am most grateful to my family, especially my parents and grandparents, who nurtured and fed my imagination through the years and pointed me to the truth from an early age. A special thank you to my sister Esther to whom this book is dedicated. We have shared so many happy memories together. I would also like to thank my girlfriend Jenna, whose love and support has been overwhelming this past year. *Danke je vel.*

Last, and not least, *Soli Deo Gloria…*

Select Bibliography

Barandiaran Irizar, Luis de (ed.), *A View from the Witch's Cave: Folktales of the Pyrenees* (Reno & Las Vegas: University of Nevada Press, 1991)

Bunyan, John, *Pilgrim's Progress* (Oxford: Oxford University Press, 2008 [1678])

Carroll, Lewis, *Alice's Adventures in Wonderland and Through the Looking Glass* (Oxford: Oxford University Press, 2009 [1865])

Cervantes, Miguel de, *Don Quixote de la Mancha* (Oxford: Oxford University Press, 2008 [1615])

Davies, Sioned, *The Mabinogion* (Oxford: Oxford University Press, 2008)

Dru, A (ed. and trans.), *The Journals of Søren Kierkegaard* (Oxford: Oxford University Press, 1938 [1848])

Harrer, Heinrich, *Seven Years in Tibet* (London: R. Hart-Davis, 1954 [1952])

The Holy Bible

Lewis, C.S., *The Complete Chronicles of Narnia* (London: Harpers Collins, 2000 [1950-1956])

Macfarlane, Robert, *Mountains of the Mind, A History of Fascination* (London: Granta, 2008 [2003])

Marquez, Gabriel Garcia, *One Hundred Years of Solitude* (London: Penguin, 2014 [1967])

Milton, John, *Paradise Lost* (Oxford: Oxford University Press, 2008 [1667])

Murray, James Erskine, *A Summer in the Pyrénées* (London: John Macrone, 1837)

Pagnol, Marcel, *The Water of the Hills* (London: Picador, 1989 [1963])

Powell, John Wesley, T*he Exploration of the Colorado River and its Canyons* (London: Penguin, 2003 [1875])

Robinson, James Harvey, (ed. and trans.), *Petrarch: The First Modern Scholar and Man of Letters* (New York: Putnam, 1898)

Simpson, Joe, *Touching the Void* (London: Jonathan Cape, 1988)

Sinclair, Iain, *Black Apples of Gower* (Toller Fratrum: Little Toller Books, 2015)

Thomas, R.S., *Collected Poems 1945 -1990* (London: J. M. Dent, 1993)

Thubron, Colin, *To a Mountain in Tibet* (London: Vintage, 2011)

Tolstoy, Leo, *War and Peace* (London: Vintage, 2011 [1869])

Whymper, Edward, *Scrambles Amongst the Alps* (London: John Murray, 1871)